T0312325

Cambridge Elements ☰

Elements in Historical Theory and Practice
edited by
Daniel Woolf
Queen's University, Ontario

PROGRESS AND THE SCALE OF HISTORY

Tyson Retz
University of Stavanger

CAMBRIDGE
UNIVERSITY PRESS

CAMBRIDGE
UNIVERSITY PRESS

Shaftesbury Road, Cambridge CB2 8EA, United Kingdom

One Liberty Plaza, 20th Floor, New York, NY 10006, USA

477 Williamstown Road, Port Melbourne, VIC 3207, Australia

314–321, 3rd Floor, Plot 3, Splendor Forum, Jasola District Centre,
New Delhi – 110025, India

103 Penang Road, #05–06/07, Visioncrest Commercial, Singapore 238467

Cambridge University Press is part of Cambridge University Press & Assessment,
a department of the University of Cambridge.

We share the University's mission to contribute to society through the pursuit of
education, learning and research at the highest international levels of excellence.

www.cambridge.org
Information on this title: www.cambridge.org/9781009011761

DOI: 10.1017/9781009026758

First published 2022

A catalogue record for this publication is available from the British Library.

ISBN 978-1-009-01176-1 Paperback
ISSN 2634-8616 (online)
ISSN 2634-8608 (print)

Progress and the Scale of History

Elements in Historical Theory and Practice

DOI: 10.1017/9781009026758
First published online: October 2022

Tyson Retz
University of Stavanger

Author for correspondence: Tyson Retz, tyson.retz@uis.no

Abstract: The idea of progress is a product of historical thinking. It is a bold interpretation of history that combines understandings of the past, perceptions of the present and expectations of the future. This Element examines the shifting scale of this past, present and future configuration from antiquity to the present day. It develops five categories that reveal the conceptual features of progress together with the philosophies of history in which they have been enmeshed, from temporal outlooks that held no notion of progress to universal histories that viewed progress as a law of nature, from speculation on the meaning and direction of history to the total rejection of all historical constructions. Global in scope and conversant with present-day debates in the theory and philosophy of history, the argument throughout is that the scale on which we conceive history plays a determining role in how we think about progress.

Keywords: progress, scale, temporality, agency, tradition

ISBNs: 9781009011761 (PB), 9781009026758 (OC)
ISSNs: 2634-8616 (online), 2634-8608 (print)

Contents

Introduction

Belief in progress long fell into disrepute. After reaching its high point in the nineteenth century, the new century quickly demonstrated humankind's ability to put its achievements to devastating ends. The word increasingly appeared in sardonic scare quotes, studies on the history of the idea abounded, and progress's critics were lauded as frequently as earlier generations had celebrated its prophets. A quarter way into the twenty-first century, there is no sign that progress is set to regain its former renown. Optimists prosper in certain circles, but pessimism is in vogue, crisis talk more pervasive than progress talk. There now seems a widespread attitude that our current day may not be the newest phase in the movement towards a better future.

Progress may have lost its lustre, but we remain in the grip of its logic and family resemblances. In its entourage are notions of development, evolution, change, order, process, advance, not to mention thorny questions of chronology, linearity, teleology and periodisation. Critical of progress as I am in the pages that follow, I must still describe this work as in some way concerned with how progress has evolved as an idea, with plotting its development through time, and I have of course thought carefully about the order in which the ideas follow from one another. I also trust that readers will make good progress through the text, which is not merely to expect that they will read from one page to the next, but that their understanding of the idea of progress will improve with every passing page. If there is one thing that progress is supposed to offer us, it is an improvement on what came before.

The promise for improvement perhaps explains the enormous political authority that progress continues to command. Under the slogan 'dare more progress', German chancellor and social democrat Olaf Scholz entered office in 2021 vowing to lead a 'progress coalition' for a German people, in his words, 'united by our belief in progress'.[1] The political appeal of progress stems largely from its *progressive* agenda, items that may today include renewable energy targets, affordable housing, legalisation of cannabis, relaxation of citizenship laws and a lowering of the voting age. It is a curious feature of contemporary political culture that one may support such goals, describe oneself as politically progressive and at the same time scoff at the idea of progress, as if it were possible to like spicy food but not spice, fashionable clothes but not fashion. By contrast, the small handful of self-titled 'progress parties' associated with the political right appear more at ease with the noun naming their vision of a better future.

The reason why left-liberal progressives have been uncomfortable with the idea of progress derives in part from its association with dubious laws of nature and the insertion of humankind into that equation. The progressive outlook has

---

[1] Stiglitz, 'If Olaf Scholz is Serious about Progress'.

endorsed change and agency while dispensing with the view that a fairer world will come into existence automatically as the end result of an ineluctable historical process. A second reason is that it is easy to point to gains that have resulted in losses in other areas. The damaging effects on the environment of fossil-fuelled industrial progress are an obvious example. A less clear-cut example is the social pressure reported by some women to meet a greater variety of expectations in the wake of the gains made in gender equality. Historians armed with their battery of counterexamples drawn from history tend to be the least inclined to subscribe to progress. A substantial proportion of them embrace relativism, holding that we can only evaluate progressive changes relative to other changes, not progress, period. With respect to examples such as the abolition of slavery, the expansion of opportunities for women and the recognition of loving relationships among members of the same sex, the pragmatic philosopher Philip Kitcher believes 'it would be grotesque' to judge the losses as being anywhere near on par with the huge advances made.[2]

Apart from the few attempts at a comprehensive treatment, the more common approach to studying the idea of progress has been to confine it to a time and place, movement or figure. Then there are the numerous studies made possible by the addition of a qualifier, so that a book on moral progress occupies a library shelf some distance away from its counterpart on scientific progress. Nor does one find gathered together the studies exploring progress in different fields of knowledge. Something akin to 'progress studies' would be needed before progress in art, progress in economics, progress in medicine and progress in philosophy constituted a common research category.[3]

If, as it has been said, all Western philosophy is but a footnote to Plato, then in the history of ideas, all discussion of progress has had to contend with J. B. Bury's century-old and hugely influential account. According to Bury, belief in progress emerged as a modern and secular substitute for the earlier religious belief in Providence. Only with the weakening of religious belief could progress come of age as a new secular faith. This new faith, Bury wrote, involved 'a synthesis of the past and a prophesy of the future'. To believe in progress was to be sure that society has moved, is moving and will continue to move in a desirable direction, and further, that this movement is the result of human activity, not an external will, godly or otherwise.[4] These were Bury's conditions for belief in progress.

Bury's secular-modern thesis was largely accepted but attracted criticism on two main fronts. First, his definition excluded from the outset the swathes of

---

[2] Kitcher, *Moral Progress*, 23.
[3] Such a call has been made for 'Progress Studies'. See Collison and Cowen, 'We Need a New Science of Progress'. I reflect on their proposal in the Epilogue.
[4] Bury, *Idea of Progress*, 2–5.

humanity who have attributed change to forces beyond purposefully acting historical agents. Seven decades after the publication of Bury's classic, Robert Nisbet was still at pains to argue that progress understood as 'unfolding cumulative advancement' (what we will call *developmental improvement* rather than progress) commanded greater influence in ancient thought than the doctrines of cycles and degeneration.[5] Similar arguments could be made for the prosperous premodern societies in which a commercial spirit flourished.

The second criticism concerned the alleged teleology of Bury's future-oriented definition, according to which progress is movement towards a desired goal. At least as far back as Herbert Butterfield's 1931 *Whig Interpretation of History*, historians have been conscious of the pitfalls of viewing the past as leading comfortably to the present-day status quo. In writings on the idea of progress that were to be part of his unfinished *Arcades Project*, the German philosopher and eclectic cultural theorist Walter Benjamin accused historians of producing history that was in fact 'fore-history', moments in the course of history that become moments of the present and 'change in their character according to whether the present is defined as a catastrophe or a triumph'.[6] To salvage its credibility, some sought to purge progress of all notion of movement and direction. A mid-twentieth-century critic viewed the relevance of the past not in the way that it manifested the direction of history, but rather in the way that it demonstrated the 'flexibility and malleability of human affairs' and furnished the 'subject matter of present decisions'.[7] On this model, progress was the sum result of solving individual problems, an approach we encounter later in the context of postwar liberals fearful of the totalitarian implications of claiming to know the direction of history.

Translated into the language of present-day historical theory, Bury's conceptual framework is not so outworn as it may seem. In the wake of the so-called temporal turn in history and the humanities and social sciences in general, it is in fact remarkably congenial to a study of the present-day meanings and implications of the idea of progress. 'How the past, present and future fit together', as Lucian Hölscher confirms, 'is today one of the principal concerns of historical theory', and when it comes to the relations between the past, present and future, François Hartog has gathered followers in asserting in the style of Martin Heidegger and Reinhart Koselleck, the German patron of conceptual history (*Begriffsgeschichte*), that the fundamental characteristic is 'the predominance of the category of the future'. In this 'regime of historicity', the 'future is the *telos*. It is the source of light illuminating the past. Time is no longer a simple classificatory principle, but rather an agent, the operator of a historical *process* –

---

[5] Nisbet, *History of the Idea of Progress*, xiii; Edelstein, *Idea of Progress in Classical Antiquity*.
[6] Smith, *Benjamin*, 65.   [7] Krieger, 'Idea of Progress', 486.

the other name, or rather the true name, for *progress*.' The new temporal sensibility that Christopher Clark believes rivals in magnitude the linguistic turns of the late twentieth century reopens and revitalises questions of future orientation and historical agency that set the initial standard for examining the idea of progress.[8]

Historians are sensing time more than ever, and the perception of movement that to Bury defined the idea of progress might now be described as perceiving oneself somewhere between the 'field of experience' and 'horizon of expect- ation'. Koselleck argued that until the French Revolution, experience and expectation were united in a way that made the past a reliable guide to the present (*historia magistra vitae*). What changed afterwards was that expect- ations of the future became detached from all that past experience could inform. 'The future', now, 'would be different from the past, and better, to boot'. In keeping with the view of progress as a secular faith, Koselleck made the crucial point that 'progress was directed towards an active transformation of this world, not the Hereafter, no matter how diverse the actual relationship between Christian expectation of the future and progress might be when registered by intellectual history'.[9] Progress came with an entire philosophy of history in tow, one that recast temporal coordinates in a way that allowed human beings to delight in the activities they believed brought them closer to an unknown though undoubtedly better future on this earth.

In addition to the focus on 'futures past', the temporal turn has also expanded the *scale* on which historians study the past. 'Big history' and 'deep history' are reactions against a perceived temporal shallowness of traditional historiography, and new approaches to world history and global history signify attempts to surpass traditional spatial demarcations. With the aid of twenty-first-century big data technologies, a hope is that we might now be able to write the kind of 'universal history' its earlier practitioners could only have speculated upon. David Armitage has declared that 'big is back'. After 'decades of aversion and neglect', across the discipline of history, 'the telescope rather than the microscope is increasingly the preferred instrument of examination', affording views of the past that make the Braudelian *longue durée* appear not so *longue* after all.[10]

The expansion of time is also the expansion of space, but scale can mean more. In the study of a particular concept, the English historian, archaeologist

---

[8] Hölscher, 'Mysteries of Historical Order', 134; Hartog, 'Modern *Régime* of Historicity in the Face of Two World Wars', 124; Clark, *Time and Power*, 4.

[9] Koselleck, *Futures Past*, 266.

[10] Armitage, 'What's the Big Idea?' 493. For an account of the alleged short termism of twentieth- century historical practice, see Guldi and Armitage, *History Manifesto*. For a response, see Cohen and Mandler, '*History Manifesto*: A Critique'. I take up their arguments in Section 5.

and philosopher of history R. G. Collingwood referred to a 'scale of forms', the members of which are so related that they embody the 'generic essence' of the concept, much as Koselleck viewed 'collective singulars' as aggregating disparate elements into basic, universalising concepts. To Ann McGrath, the deep history advocate and champion of Australian aboriginal history, the term scale 'can denote climbing up or over and separating things into layers'. What Marnie Hughes-Warrington calls 'scale switching' is to her primarily a question of ethics, 'when history makers slip seamlessly from talking about individuals to groups and back again or use little histories like blocks to build up big accounts of how the world ought to be understood'.[11] In all these senses, scale serves as a supple and multidimensional analytic category for navigating the many sides of progress.

Above all else, scale denotes a relation to distance, and in the new expanded view of the past some have asked whether we can still make out the purposefully acting agent of humanistically oriented historiography. At stake are the philological principles of a discipline founded in source criticism. This tension will be central to our account. The question behind this Element sprang from a concern that the new expanded scale of history is one through which it might be difficult to observe the human agents who, by Giambattista Vico's famous and discipline-making formulation, made history with their own hands (*verum factum*). Here I am committed to the principle that progress, if it is to be distinguished from neighbouring concepts, is the result of *purposeful human action*. Progress is change that human beings value and bring about as a consequence of the purposes they have in mind. What counts as progress is what human beings have determined to be desirable, and in that respect progress has been at the centre of history conceived as inquiry into the changing nature of human hopes, beliefs and desires. In the current climate of historical theory and practice, the question worth exploring is how history conceived on different scales both illuminates and obscures purposeful human agents living in the tension of freedom and necessity. The Element examines the idea of progress within different conceptions of history as well as how they reflect human action alongside the deep structures of society and environment.

Of course, the fact that progress involves an ascription of value raises questions over who decides what is valuable and on what terms. An attention

---

[11] Collingwood, *Essay on Philosophical Method*, 54–91; Koselleck, 'Introduction and Prefaces to the *Geschichtliche Grundbegriffe*', 13; McGrath in Aslanian et al., '*AHR Conversation* How Size Matters', 1435; Hughes-Warrington, *Big and Little Histories*, 7.

to scale helps with this dimension too. It enables us to examine both the *timescales* from which we draw our historical knowledge and the *standards of valuation* according to which we *weigh* and *apportion value* to different aspects of the past. It allows us to track back and forth along a shifting scale of past, present and future relations, between conceptions of progress and the philosophies of history in which they are enmeshed.

The Element is organised into five sections that illuminate the conceptions of history, viewed on different scales, in which beliefs about progress have been expressed. I offer not another history of the idea of progress, nor an account of the idea as expressed by this or that thinker, movement or event, but rather a mapping of its conceptual architecture. Sections 1 to 3 lay the conceptual groundwork. *No Progress* is about a time when time itself was seen to destroy things rather than improve things. Viewed on an appropriately large scale, present trends tended downwards and towards catastrophe. I distinguish belief in progress from belief in developmental improvement, meaning available vertically from meaning to be gained across a horizontal temporal plane, and point to the overall preference in ancient societies for spatial rather than temporal metaphors, prioritising stability, harmony and integration over future striving towards something better.

Absolute Progress is the forward movement of humanity visible on the scale of universal history, the lens through which clear patterns could be discerned, grand systems laid out, and progress declared a law of nature. Construing history as a series of stages, Europeans could travel to distant lands and experience themselves as witnesses to earlier stages of history, setting in train pernicious justifications for the subjugation of peoples seen to be located at inferior stages. Progress came of age when the future shifted from being viewed as predetermined and beyond the reach of human intervention to something capable of being actively constructed by purposeful action in the present.

Relative Progress deals with the repercussions of the universalistic construction of absolute progress and, in particular, with the problem of there being no agreed standards for evaluating its unevenly distributed effects. In the Darwinian world of conflict and competition, the weighing scale tilted as progress for some meant decline for others. Among the examples casting light on the unevenness and incommensurability of progress, I bring particular attention to the leadership role Japan played in the late nineteenth and early twentieth centuries to marginalised groups worldwide – African Americans, Australian aboriginals, early nationalists in India. I also consider the notion of progress as revivalist traditionalism and, in the example of the iconoclastic Chinese May Fourth Movement, examine more closely the links between progress and tradition, a theme that re-emerges later in the context of postwar reconstruction.

Everybody's Progress is an exercise in scale switching between groups and individuals, from progress achieved by collective planning to progress generated by the spontaneous order of the so-called free marketplace. For the historian-politician Jawaharlal Nehru, history was a point of reference that shifted in meaning as he went about instilling a collective sense of historical purpose and directionality. As for the individualistic market alternative, I highlight the conception or rather non-conception of history at the heart of neoliberalism. To achieve progress required the destruction of all constructions of historical directionality. By the final quarter of the twentieth century, the craving for economic growth had reached such proportions as to make statistics the prime means for charting a nation's progressive movement from past to present and setting benchmarks for future expectations.

Anti-Progress embodies the ethos of a modern-day society seemingly weary of the idea of progress. Within the discipline of history, an influential accusation is that history suffers from a crisis of short termism, and a proposed remedy is that history re-engage with present-day society by harnessing the possibilities of enlarged scales of analysis. In question is the fundamental idea that history is the story of what human beings have made with their own hands. Human beings have become viewed as geological agents and makers of all-pervasive technologies that their actions now serve. On the other hand, histories attentive to the fine grain of historical context continue to foreground human action as the site where history is made. Some of the most convincing studies subverting the idea of progress have come from historicists working on the small scale of institutional, economic and political context, those who reveal progress *as* history, as belonging to a past constellation of conditions that we should not expect to be repeated.

Readers in search of quick and easy condemnations will be hard pressed to find them. This is no repudiation of an idea that is ultimately about leaving the world a better place than we found it. Criticisms, nevertheless, are in no short supply. From the theories that saw Europeans regard non-Europeans as inhabiting earlier and less advanced stages of history to the more recent economic growth paradigm that has served as the measure of progress, it would seem that the idea of progress has much to answer for. The content provides ample opportunity to reassess our relationship with a concept that has shaped perceptions of others and set the standard for evaluating what is meaningful and worth striving towards.

1 No Progress

'The ancients had no conception of progress; they did not so much as reject the idea; they did not even entertain the idea.' These words betray a priggish self-satisfaction characteristic of the Victorian Age and what Asa Briggs described as its 'national mood of prosperity, when Britain was the world's workshop, the world's shipbuilder, the world's carrier, the world's banker, and the world's clearing-house'. The writer was Walter Bagehot, the English economist, journalist and political analyst who in 1872 applied theories of social evolution to the question of why European nations alone had possessed the ingenuity to free themselves from the 'cake of custom'. 'Oriental nations are just the same now', he went on; 'they hardly seem to have the basis on which to build, much less the material to put up anything worth having. Only a few nations, and those of European origin, advance.'[12]

Bagehot's words pique modern ears and yet his thesis, at least concerning the idea of progress in antiquity, has stood the test of further examination. J. B. Bury provided the classic account in the early twentieth century by denying the Greeks the conditions he believed were necessary to the concept (see the Introduction). The Greeks' limited recorded history supplied no evidence of a continuous series of discoveries that had led to a growth of knowledge or transformation of human life. Lacking this picture of the past, they could not expect that any such trend would continue in the future. And although Bury offered no insight into the Greek conception of human agency, it is clear from his account of cycles and degeneration that they provided a narrative structure no amount of human action could ultimately undo.

Two strategies were employed against Bury in the attempt to show otherwise. Ludwig Edelstein accepted his conditions while maintaining that, beginning with Xenophanes and other Presocratics, the Greek language conveyed them through other metaphorical expressions, namely *epidosis*, a term E. R. Dodds considered too general to qualify as progress, meaning 'increase', whether of good or evil and whether by human action or otherwise.[13] Edelstein attempted to demonstrate that there appeared in fifth-century Greek literature a distinction between 'antiquity' and 'modernity' typically identified with the emergence of a belief in the superiority of the present over the past in the seventeenth-century *querelle des anciens et des modernes*, that is, with what is often taken to mark the emergence of a strictly modern idea of progress. He also argued that science and technology had developed to such an extent as to furnish confidence in further advances in the future. This scientific optimism was also key to Robert Nisbet's attempt to illuminate the vision of unfolding cumulative advancement he observed long before the coming of modernity. The other strategy employed against Bury simply denied the plausibility of his definition. Sue Blundell argued that it is possible to speak meaningfully of the idea of progress even if

---

[12] Bagehot, *Physics and Politics*, 41–2; Briggs, *Victorian People*, 2.
[13] Edelstein, *Idea of Progress in Classical Antiquity*; Dodds, *Ancient Concept of Progress*.

it did not involve a consideration of the future, and even if divine powers were not excluded from the factors that explained human development.[14]

There is compelling evidence to consider the case for progress in at least two periods of optimism and prosperity in the ancient world. The first is Athens in the years preceding the outbreak of the Peloponnesian War in 431 BCE. The words Thucydides had Pericles speak at his funeral oration express an ardent cultural optimism as well as a belief that the Athenians considered their time and culture better than any previous. 'I doubt if the world can produce a man', extolled Pericles the statesman, general and first citizen of Athens, 'who where he has only himself to depend upon, is equal to so many emergencies, and graced by so happy a versatility as the Athenian'. These Athenians no longer needed the alluring fantasies of their poets; their power was real, demonstrated by 'mighty proofs' and left in 'imperishable monuments' that assured them 'the admiration of the present and succeeding ages'.[15] They were among the generations who had lived through a fifth-century enlightenment that saw culture developing in a positive direction and they attributed this movement to human reason and inventiveness. Xenophanes had expressed their self-satisfaction at the turn of the sixth and fifth centuries. 'Yet the gods have not revealed all things to men from the beginning', uttered the Ionian poet-philosopher, 'but by seeking men find out better in time'.[16]

Aeschylus put this pride in human achievement in the mouth of Prometheus and in so doing spawned a literary tradition of interpreting progress in either one of two ways, religiously as a manifestation of divine providence, or humanistically as an outcome of human purpose. Plato appears to have belonged to the second camp when he had Protagoras claim that even the absolute worst citizen of modern Athens was preferable to any savage.[17] What the modern citizen had that the latter did not was the ability to cultivate virtue by education. When this combined with a new importance attached to the concept of *technē* – the systematic application of intelligence to any field of human endeavour – the humanistic interpretation of progress was set to flourish. Thucydides had his Corinthian envoy warn the conservative Spartans that in politics, as in any *technē*, the latest inventions held the advantage. Plato's Hippias agreed with Socrates that the old artisans paled in comparison with those of their day. The medical writers went a step further by unlocking the future potential of the past fruits of *technē*. Hippocrates rejoiced that the discoveries made over a long

---

[14] Nisbet, *History of the Idea of Progress*; Blundell, *Origins of Civilization in Greek and Roman Thought*.

[15] Thucydides, *History of the Peloponnesian War*, 2.41.1, 4.

[16] Xenophanes, frag. 188 (Kirk et al., *Presocratic Philosophers*, 179).

[17] Plato, *Protagoras*, 327 c–d.

period were 'many and excellent' and that total discovery would follow 'if the inquirer be competent, conduct his researches with knowledge of the discoveries already made, and make them his starting-point'.[18]

Similar statements issued from the scientists of the Hellenistic Age and early Roman Empire, the second of the periods that could be said to have held to a notion of progress. Archimedes believed that by employing his method his contemporaries and successors would be able to discover additional theorems that had not yet occurred to him. Polybius noted contemporary advances in technology, expected future improvements and hoped that his historical work would have the practical value of allowing future generations to make a final judgement on Roman rule. Seneca had Posidonius the polymath praise the growth of the various manual occupations such as house building, milling and weaving while postulating the emergence of wise philosophers as 'fresh from the hands of the gods'. Seneca himself believed science to be still in its infancy. 'The day will come', he was confident, 'when time and longer study will bring to light truths at present hidden'.[19] Time would illuminate the full extent of the present generation's ignorance. Such conviction reverberated down through the first two centuries of the new millennium. Architects and astronomers recorded the rise of their respective sciences from crude beginnings while rejoicing in a new-found capacity for learning that had removed previous difficulties.

All this seems weighty testimony. And yet to regard these fragments as the exhibitions of thought of an age that believed in progress would be to exaggerate what was in fact the outlook of a thin selection of technical specialists. Juha Sihvola has characterised the attempt to rally them as evidence of an ancient belief in progress as 'a very bold interpretation of scarce fragments'. Dodds is happy to grant that the scientists spoke with a different voice from that of the philosophers, but submits that the philosophers rather than the scientists came closer to capturing the mindset of the general populace.[20] It seems reasonable to note the existence of a belief in *developmental improvement* defined as the output of a cumulative science, where the findings from previous inquiry serve as the starting point for subsequent inquiry. But we are far from a doctrine holding that time automatically brings improvements to the human condition.

As for the historians, they tended to emphasise the limitations imposed on progress by the human condition. Herodotus wrote as one who knew the

---

[18] Thucydides, *History of the Peloponnesian War*, 1.71.3; Plato, *Hippias Major*, 281d; Hippocrates, *De Prisca Medicina*, 2.

[19] Seneca, *Letters from a Stoic*, XC, 43; Seneca, *Natural Questions*, 7.25. See further Dodds, *Ancient Concept of Progress*, 18–23.

[20] Sihvola, *Decay, Progress, the Good Life?* 69; Dodds, *Ancient Concept of Progress*, 18.

instability of human prosperity, forever at the mercy of a power prohibiting humankind from rising above its station. In Thucydides the limitation was the result not of an external power but of a human nature so unalterable he felt bound to alert his readers to the unhappy probability that the events he was about to describe would happen again. From fourth-century Athens, the picture of the city's upward trajectory during the previous century may have led Aristotle to reason that there could be temporary and limited progress between catastrophes, but this only led him to the disheartening conclusion that every skill and every philosophy had probably been discovered many times over and again perished.[21]

Herodotus represented the traditional orthodoxy that human beings were the victims of envious, interfering and above all malevolent gods. The power that to him kept humankind in check was the whim of the gods whose anger brought suffering to most and, divine favour, blessings only to a handful. To set out to change that situation by imitating the gods was ill advised. Not only would it exhibit hubris, the problem would remain that what pleased one god might well enrage another. Wiser was it to follow Pindar's recommendation. 'Do not try to become Zeus', advised the Boeotian apologist for absolute adherence to aristocratic values, 'mortal things suit mortals best'. Perfect happiness was for the gods alone, and their spitefulness ensured that human beings would never be self-sufficient. Herodotus suggested that divine retribution fell upon Croesus 'because he supposed himself to be blessed beyond all other men'.[22]

When the gods withdrew from the picture, human potential remained constrained by the doctrine that human nature is essentially fixed, thus condemning human existence to an indolent eternal recurrence. Aristotle spoke for all antiquity when he stressed the value of those aspects of the world that are eternal and unchanging over those that are transitory and contingent. It was not that the ancients disregarded change; it was that they took account of change only insofar as it illuminated what was eternal.

Better yet than the scientists, philosophers and historians at uncloaking the ancient mindset is the poet-farmer Hesiod, a contemporary of Homer and the invention of the Greek alphabet in the eighth or ninth centuries. Hesiod assumes all the more significance as a spokesperson for the age when we acknowledge his debt to the Near East and in particular to what modern scholars call the wisdom literature represented from about 2500 BCE in Sumerian, Akkadian, Egyptian, Aramaic and Hebrew texts. We have in Hesiod an expositor of a Greek worldview that was in fact shaped by non-Greek influences.

---

[21] Herodotus, *Histories*, 1.5.4; Thucydides, *History of the Peloponnesian War*, 1.22.4; Aristotle, *Metaphysics*, 1074b.

[22] Pindar, *Isthmian Odes*, V, 14–16; Herodotus, *Histories*, 1.34.1.

His account of the creation of the world and the gods in the *Theogony* has been described as a Hellenised version of an oriental myth with parallels in a Hittite text of the thirteenth century and a Babylonian poem of the eleventh. Similarly, Mesopotamia is named as the source of the ideas found in the second of his poems, the *Works and Days*.[23] In common to both Eastern and Western traditions were poetic themes concerning the origin of the cosmos, the decline from a Golden Age and the necessity of labour to survive in a fallen world distant from the paradise human beings once inhabited. The idea as old as literature itself that human beings were happier in the past than in their current miserable state lacked a Greek precedent and appears to have come from Iran or Judea. The idea could be summed up as 'the older, the better'.

In the *Works and Days*, Hesiod set a gold standard for human life in the Myth of the Five Races, the tale of humankind's increasing though not uninterrupted degeneration. First was the Golden Race, when human beings lived without the necessity of labour, so plentiful were the fruits of the bountiful earth. When that ended, the Silver Race appeared and Zeus decreed that people must work. Much inferior to their golden predecessors, still they were better than the Bronze Race that came next, fierce, grotesque and given to war and violence. Then Zeus interrupted the sequence of metals by creating a Heroic Race, 'the race before our own upon the boundless earth' whose deeds were recorded at Troy and Thebes, in short, the world of Greek legend. 'Would that I did not live among this fifth race of men', Hesiod's Iron Race that is the worst of all, 'but that I died before, or that I lived after!' As Zeus destroyed the Silver and Bronze races, so Hesiod anticipated the imminent destruction of his own society.

Although Hesiod spoke of races and not ages, it is understandable that his account of the successive creation of the five races has been interpreted as a historical process of moral decay. The myth gives vivid expression to the ancient belief that present trends, when viewed on an adequately large scale, tend downwards and towards a final, though perhaps still distant, disaster. Roughly four centuries later, Plato and Aristotle still eschewed history in elucidating their conceptions of the ideal state. History could not be invoked to legitimise a political regime if the historical process ultimately led to decay and catastrophe. In fairness to Hesiod, his purpose was not to offer a diachronic description of humanity's deviation from an original gold standard. His commitment was to his own time and people. He observed the hardship surrounding him and offered in response a guide to prosperity under difficult circumstances. If the idea of progress figured in his thought, it could only mean the florescence

---

[23] West, Introduction to Hesiod's *Works and Days*, xi–xvi; Powell, *Poems of Hesiod*, 8–9.

of a static, well-organised agrarian society, the perfection of an unchanging model with moral and social orders that stood beyond time.

Indeed the novelty of the modern idea of progress is highlighted by the fact that societies far and wide in the ancient world believed that time destroyed things rather than improved them. Nowhere did this belief find expression more powerfully and with more mathematical lucidity than in India, where a perception of time as moving in endlessly recurring cycles gave birth to a complex system of world ages and cycles of creation and destruction. The far-reaching changes that transformed all spheres of social, political, economic and religious life between the fifth century BCE and fifth century CE, giving rise to Hinduism, Buddhism and Jainism, were perceived as moral and religious decline, and the proliferation of rival belief systems was explained by the arrival of a cosmically determined age of decadence. Specifically, the gradual degeneration of humankind was explained by reference to a Vedic dice game.[24] The winning throw, Krita, referred to the number four and lent its name to the first and foremost of the yugas or ages – the Golden Age and age of truth, the longest in duration at 1,728,000 years. The throw representing three provided the name of the Tretā Yuga, the second in importance, while the third throw supplied the name of the third yuga, the Dvāpara, associated with the number two. The last and worst of the yugas was called Kali, the name of the losing throw with a numerical value of one. The names thus point to an essential characteristic of the ancient Indian conception of degeneration, a descending 4–3–2–1 sequence that determined the amount of moral goodness (*dharma*) contained in each yuga. *Dharma* diminishes by one fourth as the yugas advance, so that subjects living in our present and most debased age operate with one quarter the amount of moral goodness than was available to subjects who lived during the Golden Age.

The Sanskrit epic the *Mahābhārata* held time responsible for the destruction of the earth. Time oppresses and overpowers human beings, pushing them together with destiny towards their eventual death. So intense was the concern with its destructive nature, time became a virtual synonym for death and ruin. But human beings were not to sit idly by as destiny ran its course. 'Destiny proceeds well', says the epic, 'when supplied with action, just like a fire, even if small, becomes big when fanned by wind'.[25] Time was personified as possessing a rope that entrapped human beings in a life of bondage while carrying them away to their death. The doctrines of emancipation, enlightenment and liberation central to the Indian religions, that much coveted Buddhist *nirvana*, were

---

[24] González-Reimann, *Mahābhārata and the Yugas*, 7.

[25] Quoted in González-Reimann, *Mahābhārata and the Yugas*, 30.

an effort to break free from the wheel of time and occupy a space beyond time, and thus beyond death.

In China during the same period, the picture was less that things deteriorate than that they essentially remain stable. Ge Zhaoguang suggests that the entire foundation of ancient Chinese knowledge, thought and belief was encapsulated in the saying 'Heaven is constant and unchanging, and the Dao (Way) is also constant and unchanging'.[26] The absolute stability of the human realm was guaranteed thanks to the absolute stability of the cosmos supporting it. This theory of the Unity of Heaven and the Human functioned as an unacknowledged presupposition governing every aspect of cultural and scientific life, including astronomy and calendar making, the interpretation and explanation of natural phenomena, the understanding and treatment of human physiology and psychology, the creation of imperial power, hierarchical structures and political ideologies as well as the symbolic meaning of sacrificial and ceremonial practices. It supplied the basic patterns of cities, royal palaces and the dwellings of ordinary people, the rules of popular games and the models of aesthetic beauty in art and literature. The Dao was the Way and Heaven and Unity all in one, the eternal and naturally rational order and standard for everything.

The glance eastwards from the Greco-Roman world to India and China brings into view Karl Jaspers' hugely influential notion of an 'Axial Age', a key feature in the recent turn towards big, world and universal history. Jaspers' bold attempt at historical synthesis argued that the major civilisations of the ancient world experienced a kindred 'spiritual tension' that questioned all human activity and conferred upon it a new meaning. In the period from 800 to 200 BCE, from Confucius and Lao-tse in China to the Buddha and the authors of the Upanishads in India, Zarathustra in Iran, the Hebrew prophets in Palestine, and the philosophers, poets and historians in Greece, thinking became a goal in itself and consciousness turned towards universality and transcendence. With the realisation that something extraordinary was beginning in their present, humankind became aware that 'this present was preceded by an infinite past' and so became 'conscious of belonging to a late or even a decadent age'.[27] Human ratiocination now guided debate over the nature of the cosmos, the precepts of a virtuous life, good governance and the paths of spiritual transcendence, and the conception of another world allowed the present world to be appreciated in contrast.

In spite of the emergent historical sensibility, difficulties remain when it comes to the matter of belief in progress. First among these is the fact that the ancient world tended to think in spatial rather than temporal metaphors.

---

[26] Ge, *Intellectual History of China*, 27.   [27] Jaspers, *Origin and Goal of History*, 5–6.

The Greeks took it for granted that the sphere was essential to perfection. Parmenides the so-called founder of metaphysics described Being as eternal in the full sense that it 'never was nor will be, since it is now, all together, one, continuous' before adding that it is spherical 'like the bulk of a ball well-rounded on every side, equally balanced in every direction'. Plato had no doubt that a Demiurge-creator setting out to construct a perfect universe would make it 'in the shape of a sphere, equidistant in all directions from the centre to the extremities, which of all shapes is the most perfect'. The sphere was aesthetic perfection and the model for Being, the only solid body capable of moving (by revolving) without requiring any space outside of itself to move into, and perfect simply in virtue of this fact. Marcus Aurelius, the second-century CE Stoic and Roman emperor, would later be fond of describing the perfected soul as one that had attained a spherical form, maintained by its own figure and illuminated by its own light.[28] Symbols revered by ancient cultures from across the world presupposed the completeness, uniformity, evenness and regularity of the sphere in contrast to the cragginess, irregularity and diversity loved later by romantics.

Spherical perfection entailed no forward striving, no imperfect *now* and potentially perfect future *then*. Human beings possessed a divine element within themselves and they perfected it by contemplating the ordered glory of the universe. This required a degree of asceticism, a self-discipline common to many of the world's religions and philosophies, but more important was contemplation, the path to *sophia* or wisdom. *Sophia* consisted in looking on at the world. One did better to show up to a festival as a spectator than as a participant in the games. By contemplating the mathematical order of the universe, its harmony and unity, the soul could purify and perfect itself. Plato distinguished sharply between the body and soul, suggesting that the former corrupts the latter, and in the theory of the forms made the soul perfectible by approximation with a pre-existing ideal. One looked *upward* to discover what was eternally available rather than forward to what may be available later on down the track. For all their important differences on most other matters, it is remarkable that the three major Hellenistic schools of philosophy – the Sceptics, the Epicureans and the Stoics – all agreed that peace of mind or *ataraxia* was the supreme end to be sought after.

The spiritual conditions valued in the ancient world were not to be created by purposeful future-directed action along a horizontal temporal plane. Rather, they were available *vertically* to any individual at any time, to any person who

---

[28] Parmenides, frag. 296, 299 (Kirk et al., *Presocratic Philosophers*, 249, 252); Plato, *Timaeus*, 33b; Aurelius, *Meditations*, XI 12. See further Passmore, *Perfectibility of Man*, 38–40, 75–6.

contemplated their transcendent reality. 'Whatever its various movements', the German philosopher Hermann Lotze remarked equally of the early Christian religious outlook, 'history is not fated to make such progress longitudinally, but rather in an upward direction at every single one of its points'.[29] Human beings would have to find greater delight in their own activity before the idea of progress could assume form.

2 Absolute Progress

The features missing from the ancient world were to be found in abundance with the coming of modernity. If ancient societies esteemed what was eternal and unchanging, the tremendous pace of change in the modern era shifted priority to what was in motion, in tension and in transformation. If time had meant destruction and decay, such pessimism now seemed an oddity, the attitude in all likelihood of a grouchy social misfit agitating against the mainstream and refusing to yield to common sense. If everything needed for living a good life had been available vertically by contemplation to every individual in the here and now, the best possible life was now something looming further down the track, to be worked towards in the passing of the hours, days, months and years. If the ancient world lacked a historical outlook capable of generating a confidence that past achievements would continue into the future, the universal scale of historical reflection during the modern period supplied ample evidence of advances in a positive direction. Absolute progress is the idea that progress in separate domains of human endeavour amount to overall human progress. It is a totalising conception of human history that gave rise to the belief, still with us today, that scientific and technological progress equate with moral and human progress.

In progress we are dealing with an idea that has been considered, 'for all its universality of appeal, French to the very core'.[30] It is difficult to deny, when digging for the soil that cultivated the modern conception of progress, one soon lands in French territory. It was not that others had never contemplated questions of the future direction of humanity – we have cited examples of a certain confidence in the future – but rather that the French Enlightenment supplied the intellectual conditions for systematic reflection on the concept.

Progress got its expositor during the Revolutionary Terror. While hiding from Robespierre in the winter of 1793–1794, the Marquis de Condorcet broke with the view that the different fields of human endeavour develop independently of

---

[29] Lotze (1864) quoted in Smith, *Benjamin*, 72. On the idea of progress in early Christianity, see Bernstein, *Progress and the Quest for Meaning*, 25–46.

[30] Nisbet, Introduction to Sorel's *Illusions of Progress*, v.

one another and promulgated a new form of absolutism by depicting them as a team of horses banded together collectively pushing forward towards a common goal. Condorcet formed a picture of the past demonstrating 'by reason and by evidence that no limit has been set on the perfection of the human faculties; that the perfectibility of man is really indefinite'. From this picture he had reason to believe that progress was constrained by 'no limit other than the duration of the globe on which nature has cast us. No doubt this progress could proceed more rapidly or less, but never will it be retrograde.'[31] The first systematic elaboration of progress aggregated the different fields of human endeavour in what Reinhart Koselleck would call a 'collective singular'. 'Separate advances in one or another field now were lumped together as *progress*', much as the plural *liberties* or privileges derived from a position in the former social order of estates became the singular *liberty* common to all.[32] Viewed on the scale of an enlightened abstract universalism, progress meant history itself, the forward movement of humanity from past to present and towards the future. Its distended and generalising optics laid out a smooth passage for the realisation of humankind's unlimited potential.

A different Frenchman has marked the beginnings not in France but in the thoroughgoing empiricism of the Scottish Enlightenment and its stadial theory of history. Jacques Le Goff, the renowned authority on the twelfth and thirteenth centuries, regards the appearance of Adam Smith's *Wealth of Nations* in 1776 as the decisive turning point that ended what he terms the 'long middle ages' by elevating the status of commercial society to prime rank as the engine powering humanity in its desired direction. By Le Goff's account, the Middle Ages can be distinguished from the modern period precisely by their lack of a notion of progress. 'Like a seal set on the state of mind of a society that was at last breaking with the Middle Ages and becoming truly modern, the word *progress* was employed.' Although the Middle Ages were 'constantly alert to novelty, a harbinger of the idea of progress', they were different in the fundamental respect that they did not connect human flourishing with the forward movement of society towards an ever-increasing perfection.[33] Heinz Arndt believes the idea is difficult to identify much before the eighteenth century. 'Medieval man, expecting little from his brief span in this vale of tears, sought – or at any rate was urged to seek – the salvation of his soul', not strive towards something better. By the crude indicator of economic growth, Robert Gordon does not hesitate to set the date at 1770.[34]

---

[31] Condorcet, *Outlines of an Historical View of the Progress of the Human Mind*, 11.

[32] Koselleck, 'Introduction and Prefaces to the *Geschichtliche Grundbegriffe*', 13.

[33] Le Goff, *Must We Divide History into Periods?* 102–3.

[34] Arndt, *Rise and Fall of Economic Growth*, 5; Gordon, *Rise and Fall of American Growth*, 2.

Le Goff's reading is consistent with the conventional interpretation of the Scottish philosopher and economist as a prophet of commercialism and what we know today as free-market capitalism. Smith's canonical status as a founder of modernity rests on a view that commercial society is the variety of economic organisation most capable of satisfying the ends of human nature. These ends Smith identified as self-preservation, order, happiness, procreation of the species and perfection of the species. He believed less that human beings act purposefully to bring about these ends than that nature has endowed human beings with instincts and passions naturally inclining them to their realisation. Smith viewed the historical process teleologically in the sense that it culminated in a society that had completed the path of history along four stages, from the Age of Hunters, the Age of Shepherds, the Age of Agriculture and finally to the Age of Commerce, with each age representing a more advanced state of society than the previous one. The 'natural progress of improvement' was the 'natural course of things' and 'promoted by the natural inclinations of man'.[35] Only in the commercial stage, with its growing wealth, prosperity, cosmopolitanism and widening of the sphere of moral sentiments, could the members of a society cultivate themselves and their institutions in ways consistent with the ends of human nature.

JoEllen DeLucia has coined the term 'stadial fiction' to describe popular novels that recounted the journeys of heroines through the various environments illustrative of the different stages of historical development.[36] These novels contrasted the aesthetic sensibilities of different nations and shifted discussion of historical development from men and economics to women and matters of taste. The eighteenth century was, after all, the Age of Sensibility as much as it was the Age of Commerce. David Hume mapped women's contributions to the refinement of sentiment onto the progress of knowledge, and John Millar went further than most in recognising the value of 'female accomplishments and virtues which have so much influence upon every species of improvement, and which contribute in so many different ways to multiply the comforts of life'.[37] DeLucia reveals that the controversy over the authenticity of the Ossianic poems (1760–1763), hugely popular in Scotland and internationally, offered educated women an opportunity to join the conversation on the nature of change, progress and modernity. These women were relatively untroubled by the question of whether the poems were authentic and instead embraced inauthenticity and hybridity 'to craft associations that unsettled

---

[35] Smith (1776) quoted in Alvey, 'Adam Smith's View of History', 5.

[36] DeLucia, *Feminine Enlightenment*, 157–65.

[37] Hume, 'Rise of the Arts and the Progress of Science', 134; Millar, *Origin of the Distinction of Ranks*, 108. See further O'Brien, *Women and Enlightenment in Eighteenth-Century Britain*.

standard national, political, and familial frameworks'.[38] The poems depicted a third-century society in which feminine refinement of manners and delicacy of sentiment combined with masculine virtues of public spirit and military valour. The florescence of sensibility in so primitive a society violated the stadial theory of historical development. Following the example of the poems, women writers subverted the claim that material progress necessarily ennobles the human spirit.

Smith's theory of the four stages seems a plain example of history conceived as smooth, uninterrupted linear progress. But like many thinkers whose vision was vast and output voluminous, Smith does not always pass the test of internal consistency. Observable across his œuvre are dark patches where he appears to imply cycles and degeneration. Robert Heilbroner has argued that Smith left us with a 'deeply pessimistic prognosis' in which material decline awaits us at the end of the historical journey and moral decay is suffered by society in its course.[39] Readers of Smith are thus faced with a decision regarding his conception of history. On the one hand, the linear movement to commercial society implies the 'end of history', the final arrival at a diversified and resource-rich terminus providing the necessary conditions for human flourishing. On the other hand, the nature of work in this stationary state deadens the intellect, stifles creativity and reduces the vibrancy of civic life, leading ultimately to social decay and raising the suspicion that Smith's final stage of the historical process is in fact one caught up in a cyclical process of rise and decline. We may be satisfied along with James Alvey that the final evaluation of Smith's conception of history depends in large part on how one weighs his varied statements on 'either side of the optimism/pessimism scale'.[40] The old idea of historical decline or decay lingered in eighteenth-century Britain among cultural primitivists who emphasised the aesthetic, moral and physical advantages of the 'natural' over the 'refined', among critics of the allegedly pernicious effects of commercial society, and among those who saw in the excessive accumulation and enjoyment of wealth a downward trajectory analogous to that suffered by Rome.[41]

An important influence on the eighteenth century was a writer who alleged to the contrary that an individual's desire to live in material comfort produced results beneficial to the whole of society. Bernard Mandeville, the Anglo-Dutch philosopher, political economist and satirist, recounted in *The Fable of the Bees* the story of a beehive where 'every Part was full of Vice, Yet the whole Mass a Paradise'.[42] The society of bees flourished until Jove, their god, moved to

---

[38] DeLucia, *Feminine Enlightenment*, 191.   [39] Heilbroner, 'Paradox of Progress', 243.

[40] Alvey, 'Adam Smith's View of History', 20.

[41] Spadafora, *Idea of Progress in Eighteenth-Century Britain*, 14.

[42] Mandeville, *Fable of the Bees*, 24.

eliminate vice from the hive. Newly virtuous and no longer driven to compete with one another, the bees' industry collapsed and the formerly prosperous society met its demise in a battle. For all its scandalous implications, which mocked long-standing traditions of Christian and republican asceticism, Mandeville had a clear message – human vices were the main engines of the collective good. Remove vanity, for example, and the fashion industry collapses, resulting in mass unemployment, economic downturn and the possible reduction of the military power of the British commercial state. 'Private vice, public benefit' conveyed a principle of human nature that individuals barter and trade for private advantage, which by generating economic growth propels commercial society forwards. It has even been speculated that Mandeville's slogan was the source of Smith's 'invisible hand', for he introduced the now well-known tenet of free-market economics while discussing an act of private gain that had produced an unintended public benefit.

The English republican historian and radical Catharine Macaulay took issue with the idea promoted by Mandeville that human beings are naturally self-interested. She defended the thesis that there are immutable moral truths, accessible to human reason, that lead to social progress. Mandeville's doctrine made the prospect of moral improvement, by which Macaulay meant social progress, appear chimerical. She defended an account of liberty that did not equate with mere licence. This was her doctrine of moral necessity according to which freedom does not consist in arbitrary decision but rather in the will to act in accordance with the judgement of what is best. Humanity's potential for moral improvement depended on the extent to which the growth of reason sculpts the freedom of the will.[43]

Karen Green has discussed Macaulay along with other female friends of Enlightenment universalism and progress. Marie-Charlotte-Pauline de Lezadière presented to Louis XVI a political history of the French monarchy that the king sat on for over a decade and sent to the press only when, in the Revolutionary turmoil of the early 1790s, he recognised its potential to establish the foundations of the crown's authority. Louise-Félicité de Keralio also took an interest in the limits of monarchical power, but from a more critical perspective than Lezadière and through an account of a period of English history during which women played a prominent role.[44]

Where there were optimists, there were pessimists lurking in the corner. In a century giddy with the prospects for progress, Jean-Jacque Rousseau knew he held the minority position. He readied himself for 'universal outcry' in 1750

---

[43] Macaulay, *Treatise on the Immutability of Moral Truth*.
[44] Green, *History of Women's Political Thought in Europe*, 179–80, 205.

when he argued to the Academy of Dijon, one of Europe's most learned scientific societies, that 'our souls have been corrupted to the extent that our sciences and our arts have advanced towards perfection'. Condorcet looked on with disbelief at the persistence of such pessimism, of those lovers of paradox who complained about 'the decadence of knowledge even when actually it was progressing'. The Catholic apologist Louis-Antoine de Caraccioli put the matter more strongly when he wrote in 1759 that the eighteenth century had so far offered its successors nothing 'but insipid novels, miserable plays, impious philosophies, and extravagant opinions. How corrosive this degeneration has been!'[45] Following the intellectual discoveries of Descartes, Newton and Leibniz, the eighteenth century could appear in comparison to have downgraded itself to a crude journalism and popularisation prohibiting serious thought. The revolution in empirical science offered proof that actuality did not measure up to ideal, and nor would it, many believed, in the future. As easily as rationalist philosophy could postulate the forward movement of civilisation, so historical analogies with the fall of Rome and the presumed 'dark' Middle Ages could depict decadence as the true universal governing the historical process.

Projects launched from the 1750s by physicists and philosophers sought to combat the various forms of degeneration they believed stained France. William Max Nelson has argued that a major temporal reorientation had to take place before such regenerative action could even be contemplated. Before mid-century, Nelson explains, the concept of 'preformation' or pre-existence still committed Europeans to a deterministic outlook.[46] Thinkers of all persuasions were in general agreement that time was an unfolding from one predetermined state to another. Human beings could work individually and collectively to refine these states – they could improve them over time – but thwarting their efforts to bring about more lasting, large-scale transformation was the doctrine that nature is regular, stable and returns an identical image of itself. The present was thought to contain a multi-layered seed from which the future unfolded, or in Leibniz's phrase, 'the present is pregnant with the future'.[47] Nature had imprinted its eternal code on the passage of time, and passivity remained the most sensible stance to adopt towards a predetermined future beyond the reach of human intervention.

When irregularities were occasionally observed, the problem was often explained as one of scale. If only the irregularity were viewed from a 'higher' vantage point, then one would observe more elements, longer stretches of

---

[45] Rousseau, *First Discourse*, 51; Condorcet (1795) quoted in Vyverberg, *Historical Pessimism in the French Enlightenment*, 75; Caraccioli, *La jouissance de soi-même*, ix.

[46] Nelson, *Time of Enlightenment*, 21–3.

[47] Leibniz used this phrase in a number of works. See Nelson, *Time of Enlightenment*, 163 (n. 5).

continuity, and thereby grasp the ultimate uniformity of the seemingly different images of nature moving through time. The concept of preformation, then, had to be dislodged before society could regenerate itself.

Pivotal in this respect was the naturalist Georges-Louis Leclerc de Buffon, an early admirer of 'deep time' and architect of the doctrine, critical to the decades that were to come, that human beings can undo what time has done and actively construct the future. Buffon achieved fame in the 1770s with the provocative claim that the earth was just under seventy-five thousand years old, in contrast to previous estimations from biblical sources of around six thousand years. As he and like-minded naturalists and philosophers opened up deep time behind them, they also searched for the natural laws, mechanisms and processes that might enable them to shape the development of living beings in the future. Buffon transformed the meaning of Leibniz's phrase to a pregnancy whose outcome human beings could now directly influence. His living beings were domestic animals, 'biological instruments of futurity' that in his experiments in selective breeding demonstrated that living organisms were not fated to degenerate. On the contrary, individuals of a particular lineage did not develop strictly according to the 'original prototype' of their species. That very prototype could be altered and improved.[48]

Buffon serves as an example that a temporal reorientation towards the future recast the present as the site where human beings could now actively construct a future fundamentally different from the past. The example is crucial when we remind ourselves that progress is a theory that not only delights in human activity, but more specifically in the ability of human beings to act in the present to create a future better than the past. It presupposes connections between the past, present and future in the absence of which human effort in the here and now could never be conceived as a forward-moving constructive project. Buffon along with other physiocrats in the second half of the eighteenth century assumed that conditions in the moral, social and political spheres were chiefly a result of conditions in the physical or material sphere. The idea that '*le physique* determines *le moral*' provided a successful springboard for action and constructing the future.[49] With every new discovery and manipulation of the natural world, they constructed a better future for humanity.

As in the Scottish Enlightenment, the trajectory along which this placed humanity was understood in the French Enlightenment as a single path through three or four stages of human development. While sketching plans for a universal history in 1751, Smith's counterpart in France, Anne-Robert-Jacques Turgot, marvelled that a 'glance over the earth puts before our eyes,

---

[48] Nelson, *Time of Enlightenment*, 29, 95–120.   [49] Nelson, *Time of Enlightenment*, 15.

even today, the whole history of the human race, showing us traces of all the steps and monuments of all the stages through which it has passed from the barbarism, still in existence, of the American peoples to the civilisation of the most enlightened nations of Europe'. The differences between peoples throughout the world were differences in the extent to which the different modes of subsistence (hunting and gathering, pasturage, agriculture, commerce) provided for human flourishing.

Planted in the minds of European *voyageur-philosophes*, to observe distant societies at earlier stages of development was thus to witness people living in the past. The savant and statesman Joseph-Marie Degérando wrote to the members of the Baudin expedition to Australia in 1800 that the 'philosophical traveller, sailing to the ends of the earth, is in fact travelling in time; he is exploring the past; every step he makes is the passage of an age'. To travel through space was to travel through time. By the same token, when these Europeans returned home to Europe, they experienced themselves as living in the future. Nelson refers to this as an instance of 'simultaneous non-simultaneity' (the *Gleichzeitigkeit des Ungleichzeitigen*), as having available to human experience the different stages of human development at one and the same time.[50] Believing themselves to be located in a more advanced stage of history, Europeans were poised to recount triumphant histories of modern nations while looking back regrettably on those peoples stranded in the earlier stages. The 'real problem of history', to the German poet and philosopher Friedrich Schlegel, was precisely this 'inequality of progress in the various elements of human development; in particular, the great divergence in the degree of intellectual and ethical development'.[51]

There are pernicious signs here, indeed, an entire temporal template for 'bringing civilisation' to peoples at lesser stages of historical development. It was those who possessed the foresight to actively construct the future who were modern, developed and civilised, while those who were seen to attend solely to their immediate needs languished in a backward and perpetual present. Rousseau and later Kant expressed this prejudice with all too harmful and lasting an influence in their remarks about the inhabitant of the Caribbean who in the morning sells his hammock, only to find in the evening that he has nowhere to sleep.[52]

The events of 1789 are typically seen as the turning point that broke with the past and ushered in what we now call modern history. Alexis de Tocqueville

---

[50] Meek, *Turgot on Progress, Sociology and Economics*, 89; Degérando, *Observation of Savage Peoples*, 63; Nelson, *Time of Enlightenment*, 40–3.

[51] Schlegel (1795) quoted in Koselleck, *Futures Past*, 266.

[52] Rousseau, *Second Discourse*, 98; Kant, 'Anthropology from a Pragmatic Point of View', 294. See further Nelson, *Time of Enlightenment*, 49–58.

recognised that no nation had ever before attempted 'to break with the past, to make, as it were, a scission in their life line and to create an unbridgeable gulf between all they had hitherto been and all they now aspired to be'. The forces of tradition were stopped in their tracks, the rights of men were declared, citizens seized authority, and the Napoleonic exportation of universalistic principles sparked national movements that made historians the romantic seers of every nation's past and the privileged expositors of every nation's collective consciousness. The French Revolution gave birth to the modern nation and to modern historical consciousness, the knowledge that every nation had a distinct national past that gave it a distinct national identity contained within distinct national borders. But although Tocqueville acknowledged that the French 'spared no pains in their endeavour to obliterate their former selves', their efforts were ultimately futile, for they had 'used the debris of the old order to build up the new'.[53] Why had they failed to achieve the progress so many thought they had? In the style of nineteenth-century historiography, Tocqueville took the nation as the prime unit of analysis. No amount of revolutionary transformation had so far been sufficient to allay the impulse to centralisation of state power deeply engrained in the French national character.[54]

Tocqueville offered this assessment midway through a nineteenth century lined with formidable thinkers on progress. Among them were the system builders whom Frank Manuel called the 'prophets of Paris' – Turgot, Condorcet, Saint-Simon, Fourier and Comte – whose philosophical history attempted to discern an absolute system that would dictate the rules of the future new order. So bent were they on seeing in history a plan for the future, the English liberal and utilitarian philosopher John Stuart Mill had to ask 'why this universal systematising, systematising, systematising? Why is it necessary that all human life should point to one object, and be cultivated into a system of means to a single end?'[55] Mill had in mind Comte's positive science of a High Priest of Humanity who, while synthesising the past, would bequeath to humankind a unity of movement and purpose unruffled by the petty commotions of the moment. Philosophical history was necessary for sound prophecy, and prophecy laid the foundation of sound social conduct. When Bury in the early twentieth century elaborated what constituted belief in progress, he looked back admiringly on these system builders, the bearers of the secular faith of progress, on their ambitious fusion of past, present and future, their conviction that history held the key to the future and their commitment not merely to contemplating history but actively determining its direction.

---

[53] Tocqueville, *Old Régime and the French Revolution*, vii.
[54] Slaboch, 'Tocqueville's Philosophy of History', 94.
[55] Mill (1865) quoted in Manuel, *Prophets of Paris*, 249.

In spite of the number and diversity of nineteenth-century thinkers, theories, systems, movements and schools, and in spite of the examples of several devout pessimists and the enduring preoccupation with decay and degeneration that must figure into any evaluation of progress, the nineteenth century tended to replicate the eighteenth century in three principal ways.[56] Convictions remained that progress is a law of nature, that progress is to be gauged according to different stages of human development, and that universal history is the scale on which all this is visible.

Near the end of the eighteenth century, Kant placed emphasis on this last point in arguing that history, 'if it examines the free exercise of the human will *on a large scale*', revealed a hidden plan of nature to achieve a political order and constitution in which humankind's capacities could be fully realised.[57] Nothing less than universal history could illuminate the 'cosmopolitan purpose' guided by reason that nature had imbued in humankind. It was useless to attempt to discern reason realising itself in the lifetime of individuals; only in the entire species did reason objectify itself. In a short essay on progress, Kant suggested that to discern progress required looking beyond experience to humankind's moral character. He knew full well that human beings seldom displayed their best moral selves, and he expected little of them. But they had nature on their side. Rather than impeding progress, the mutual antagonisms between peoples were in fact nature thrashing out the terms of a republican order and a 'perpetual peace' guaranteed by international law.[58]

Idealism is the philosophical doctrine that the ideas we have structure our experience of reality. Names such as Kant, Fichte, Schelling and Hegel belong to the idealist school insofar as they put mind before matter in coming to terms with the fundamental nature of reality.[59] Hegel was the first philosopher to argue strongly in favour of history because he regarded it the work of philosophy to discover in history the growing realisation of rational organisation and freedom. 'History', after all, 'is mind clothing itself with the form of events or the immediate actuality of nature. The stages of its development are therefore presented as immediate natural principles.' The 'cunning of reason' was such that human beings did not make history but rather helped reason make it. Progress revealed itself in the developing emancipation of rational character, the process by which reason strove towards its ends, expressed in actions that

---

[56] On nineteenth- and twentieth-century sceptics of the idea of progress, see Slaboch, *Road to Nowhere*.

[57] Kant, 'Idea for a Universal History with a Cosmopolitan Purpose', 41.

[58] Kant, 'Contest of Faculties', 177–90; Kant, 'Perpetual Peace', 93–130.

[59] Readers of German may wish to consult the extensive '*Fortschritt*' entry to Koselleck and colleagues' *Geschichtliche Grundbegriffe*, 351–423.

are 'the living instruments of what is in substance the deed of the world mind'.[60] Much to the discredit of his philosophy of history, Hegel presented this advance of reason as universal history advancing westwardly, from the despotic oriental realm in the east to the liberated Germanic realm in the west. When Leopold von Ranke famously implored historians to study the past 'as it actually happened', he was protesting against this *a priori* imposition of the meaning and direction of history. In opposition to Hegel's natural-law inspired philosophical school, Ranke's historical school went on to establish history as an autonomous form of knowledge working in the service of fledgling nineteenth-century nation states.

Dialectical idealism was Hegel's way of explaining how ideas come into conflict and give rise to new ideas. Where there is no friction, there is no history. The dialectic operated according to the view that a *thesis* is met with an *antithesis*, the resolution of which produces a *synthesis* that forms the new thesis, and so on and so on. Karl Marx saw merit in the dialectic but objected to the notion that mind comes before matter. The food on one's plate said more about one's situation than the ideas running through one's head. Dialectical materialism retained the logic of Hegel's idea of progress but turned it on its head. 'My dialectical method', wrote Marx, 'is not only different from the Hegelian, but is its direct opposite . . . the ideal is nothing else than the material world reflected by the human mind, and translated into forms of thought'.[61] History to followers of Marx became the dynamic interplay of human beings and their natural environment, where ways of life and social order were determined by the mechanics of the economic environment, and where people and societies themselves changed as material conditions changed.

In the first decade of the twentieth century, the voluntarist Marxist and Frenchman Georges Sorel complained that the material comfort many Europeans now enjoyed made progress nothing more than a decadent bourgeois ideology of political passivity.[62] Why act at all, he asked, if progress automatically makes the world a better place? The idea of progress had lulled nineteenth-century society into believing that a law of nature would do the work for them.

Sorel was writing at a time when the inequities of the enlightened conception of absolute progress were beginning to show. Those excluded from its ineluctable advances would have to close in the gap themselves. In Russia, a young Vladimir Lenin engaged in a debate about the applicability of the Marxist dialectic to Russia's relatively backward economy.[63] His opponents in the

---

[60] Hegel, *Philosophy of Right*, 346, 348. The concluding sections of this work offer an outline of Hegel's program in his *Philosophy of History*.
[61] Marx, *Capital*, 10–11.   [62] Sorel, *Illusions of Progress*.
[63] Melnik, 'Lenin as a Development Economist', 37–9.

1890s were the Narodniks who believed that the capitalist stage of the dialectic could be circumvented, and the Russian people delivered directly to the final stage, agrarian socialism. Lenin on the other hand sought to uphold the Marxist orthodoxy and argued that Russia had already in fact entered into the capitalist stage. Lenin's side succeeded in controlling the Marxist narrative and in portraying their opponents as home-grown eccentrics out of touch with the 'modern theory' from the West. The main communist movement of the early twentieth century, Marxism–Leninism acknowledged the progressiveness of capitalist development all while remaining confident that its inherently profound social contradictions would fuel the transition to a new and more advanced stage.

In the light of social and political experience, the grand theoretical systems built on the foundations of the Enlightenment's abstract universalism showed cracks. The absolute progress of humankind illuminated by universal history was, in the end, a philosophical construction. History viewed on the smaller scale of the more recent past made clear that, whatever progress had been achieved, it had been anything but evenly distributed. The inherent relativity of the idea of progress meant that every group would have to tilt the weighing scale in its own direction.

3 Relative Progress

If progress consists in the belief that society has moved, is moving and will continue to move in a desirable direction, then it involves an *ascription of value*. Viewed on the scale of universal history, nature provided the lens for viewing humankind's forward movement through time. As nature tended to itself self-sufficiently, so human beings perfected themselves in the natural unfolding of historical progress.

Beyond Europe, were the concepts that came with modernity choices that people could exercise or did they provide the fundamental conditions of choice? David Scott has argued that the 'tragedy of colonial enlightenment' is partly that the latter proved the case: non-Europeans were 'conscripts' rather than 'volunteers' of modernity.[64] It was less that they chose from an open range of alternatives than that modernity made possible only a certain sample of alternatives. Relative progress is progress pursued on this uneven playing field. It reflects a world of competing interests as progress for some portends decline for others. Michael Ruse describes absolute progress as progress without qualification, so directed is it at an end result that everyone by and large considers desirable. 'If one arrives at the Heavenly City', he writes, 'one has made absolute progress. If one makes a bigger and better atom bomb', on the other

---

[64] Scott, *Conscripts of Modernity*, 98–131.

hand, 'one has made comparative progress'.[65] Comparative progress involves qualification, a weighing of pros and cons as they bear upon the lives of different groups and individuals disproportionately. I call this relative progress insofar as it is an evaluation conducted from the standpoint of different groups or collectivities.

R. G. Collingwood outlined the problem of applying a standard of valuation in the example of a community of fish eaters who one day develop a method for doubling their daily catch. Does the increase in supply signify progress? The younger generation may have reason to believe so. They could work the same number of hours as before and enjoy double the amount of fish to eat, or they could get by on the previous amount and enjoy half a day's leisure. But the older generation whose social and religious associations are rooted in the old method were sure to consider the new method a decadence threatening the traditional way of life that the community knew and valued. The example served Collingwood to illustrate that progress can be said to have occurred only when there is *gain without corresponding loss*. 'If there is any loss, the problem of setting gain against loss is insoluble.' Moreover, 'progress is not a mere fact to be discovered by historical thinking; it is only through historical thinking that it comes about at all'.[66] To ascertain that the solving of an old problem created no new problems is to evaluate the relative value of two ways of life. The weighing of progress alongside tradition is a recurrent theme of this section.

Even the theory of evolution that came on the back of progress is hopelessly relativistic. At first glance, evolution may appear to belong to our previous section on progress as a law of nature. After all, we know Charles Darwin as the person who announced in 1859 the existence of a 'general law, leading to the advancement of all organic beings, namely, multiply, vary, let the strongest live and weakest die'. 'I mean by Nature', he added later, 'only the aggregate action and product of many natural laws, and by laws the sequence of events as ascertained by us'.[67] The sequence of events as ascertained by Darwin did not necessarily imply progressive development. What survives in one situation may not survive in another. Adaptation to environment produces variations that demand their own evaluative standards. Darwin's fluid and changeable world succeeded Newton's mathematically ordered universe, and with it a common standard for evaluating progress.

Viewed on the scale of evolution, variability, adaptation and extinction demonstrated to Darwin that the future remained open to becoming what human beings could not foresee. Evolution offered an alternative philosophy

---

[65] Ruse, *Monad to Man*, 20.   [66] Collingwood, *Idea of History*, 324–7, 329, 333.
[67] Darwin, *Origin of Species by Means of Natural Selection*, 85.

of history to that of the Christian awaiting the promised *telos*.[68] Unlike other big generalists – Hegel, Comte, Marx, Spencer – Darwin forbade belief that human beings arrive at a final stage of development or even have an end in sight. J. C. Levenson has argued that writing history in the age of Darwin meant viewing topics not as singular and self-contained 'species', but rather as what Darwin termed 'varieties', a grouping that brought new attention to the multiplicity of relations contained in individual units of analysis. Thus a work such as Henry Adams' 1889 *History of the United States* could in the manner of Darwin narrow in on short four-year presidential administrations, avow its limitations as merely political history, and nevertheless require nine volumes to illuminate the general themes running through its mass of intricate details. History, as in the world of *The Origin of Species*, became flux and multiplicity, where novelties constantly sprang up and phenomena slid irrevocably into extinction.[69] Gone were the eternal recurrences of the classical world and the orderly uniformities of the enlightened world.

That evolution is an uneven process could imply that it sets up competition between groups. At least this seems to be the legacy of social Darwinism understood as the application of Darwin's biological theories to the understanding of human society. A widespread and seemingly straightforward way of defining social Darwinism has been to invoke a series of catchphrases depicting the world as a theatre of conflict – 'struggle for existence', 'survival of the fittest' and the more benign sounding but no less merciless 'natural selection'.[70] Benjamin Kidd, a self-educated clerk turned populariser of evolutionary theory, put it bluntly that 'it is an inevitable law not only that competition and selection must accompany progress, but that they must prevail amongst every form of life which is actually not retrograding'.[71] The constant struggle among individuals for resources, status and esteem explained to Kidd the dominant position of the West in the progress of civilisation.

Evolutionary theories resonated with Europeans who considered themselves superior to the native inhabitants of the Americas, Africa, Asia and Australasia. We considered earlier the notion that returning to Europe from these lands was to travel from the past back into the future. Now in the second half of the nineteenth century, there was wide acceptance of the idea that races were distinct, biologically determined types that could be ranked along a scale of inferiority and superiority, with those at the bottom of the hierarchy posing a danger to those at the top. Clémence Royer took it upon herself in the preface

---

[68] See Ruse, *Evolution as Religion*.
[69] Levenson, 'Writing History in the Age of Darwin', 119–23.
[70] Hawkins, *Social Darwinism in European and American Thought*, 3–4.
[71] Kidd, *Social Evolution*, 41.

of her French translation of the *Origin* to caution that human races 'are clear-cut and highly unequal varieties; and it is necessary to think twice before claiming political and civic equality in a people composed of a minority of Indo-Germans and a majority of Mongolians or Negroes'.[72] Races were subject to natural selection because they were engaged in a struggle for existence. In an imperialistic Europe, that meant first and foremost a struggle for territory. As for preserving and improving moral and social conditions within industrial Europe's mush-rooming towns and cities, supporters of eugenics shared the view that the survival of the national or racial community came before any consideration of individual rights.

Such attitudes explain the shock felt globally in 1905 when Japan defeated Russia in the first major conflict of the twentieth century and what is frequently characterised as the first victory of an Asian people over a European people. Japan had only recently learnt that nations not poised for offence were likely to be dominated by those that were. *Sakoku* or the 'locked country' was the isolationist foreign policy of the Tokugawa shogunate (1603–1868) that had severely limited relations and trade with the outside world, barred foreign nationals from entering the country and kept ordinary Japanese from leaving it. Only with the news of the First Opium War in China in the 1840s did alert samurais become aware of the supremacy of Western military technology, and only with the arrival of an American naval squadron in Tokyo Bay in 1853 – Commodore Matthew C. Perry's famous 'gunboat diplomacy' that led to the signing of unequal treaties with the United States, Russia, Britain, France and Holland – did the disparity between East and West become apparent to ordinary Japanese.

Once realised, no country modernised more speedily and embraced more one-dimensionally the doctrine that progress is to be measured by the simple criterion of that which wins. The Japanese word for progress was coined from neo-Confucian antecedents and was soon adapted into the Chinese language. Faced with the threat of Western subjugation, it was progress or perish, or progress for survival. The moral and ethical progress of humankind in the style of Condorcet was an irrelevance. One did not generalise from the technological-scientific sphere to the human-moral sphere. Progress meant the ability to compete in the international arena. The idea imported the value system of Western imperialism, not the philosophy of the Enlightenment.[73]

Although progress in the Japanese conception implied no totalising philoso-phy federating the different branches of human endeavour, it was not free of

---

[72] Royer, Preface to *De l'origine des espèces*, lxix. See further Hawkins, 'Social Darwinism and Race', 224–35.
[73] Nakayama, 'Chinese "Cyclic" View of History vs. Japanese "Progress"', 73.

ideology. Government-led efforts at industrialisation were situated within a discourse of *bunmei kaika* that encouraged all members of Japanese society to attain a level of civilisation and enlightenment equal to that of the West. Meiji leaders toured Europe and the United States, hired foreign investors to speed along the modernisation process and sent students abroad who eventually replaced the foreign tutors. By the 1890s, Japan had a new form of government, a rapidly growing industrial sector, transportation and communications infrastructure, a new system of public education, a military establishment and diplomatic relations with foreign powers that led to the revision of the unequal treaties. As David Wittner has observed, a Victorian attitude towards progress and material culture sat behind these developments.[74] 'Progress ideology' infused cultural value into materials deemed modern, which in turn generated beliefs in the inevitably of technological progress for the betterment of society. Icons of the Industrial Revolution – cast iron and steam engines, coal and bricks – were materials that symbolised modernity and progress. Described by words such as sturdy and permanent, a society that had brick buildings and iron bridges, railroads and telegraph networks, was modern and civilised. Embedded in modern materials were the values on which the new nation constructed itself.

Japan's success served as an example to marginalised groups across the world. Specifically, Marc Gallicchio has argued that the Japanese defeat of the Russian Pacific Fleet is the starting point for tracing the development of 'black internationalism' in the African American community. The 'Negro reaction' to Japan's victory at Port Arthur was one of amazement and hope. Here were a people of colour triumphing over a European imperialist power. Black activists such as Marcus Garvey, W. E. B. Du Bois and Booker T. Washington thought Japan might lead a worldwide liberation movement for people of colour. Washington told a Japanese editor that the 'wonderful progress of the Japanese and their sudden rise to the position of one of the greatest nations of the world has nowhere been studied with greater interest or enthusiasm than by the Negroes of America'.[75] Japan strengthened its status even further as the leader of the non-white world when it requested a racial equality clause in the charter of the League of Nations, a request that was ultimately denied.

The activist Marcus Garvey was a Jamaican who established in Harlem in 1918 the Universal Negro Improvement Association (UNIA). With an estimated four million members at the height of its influence in the early 1920s, it was the largest black movement ever assembled in the United States.

---

[74] Wittner, *Technology and the Culture of Progress in Meiji Japan*, 4–10.

[75] Washington (1912) quoted in Gallicchio, *African American Encounter with Japan and China*, 14.

Garvey's success stemmed largely from the way he tied together in glowing style Negro triumphs of the past and the glories he believed awaited them in the future. These narratives he disseminated in a highly successful and internationally circulated newspaper, the *Negro World*. Its weekly issues took to every corner of the globe Garvey's program for bettering the industrial, commercial, religious and political conditions of people of colour everywhere. Besides domestic admirers such as Elijah Muhammed, Malcolm X and Martin Luther King, the future Vietnamese leader Ho Chi Minh developed a close connection with the UNIA. As a seaman in his youth, Ho spent several months in New York, observed with interest the rise of Garvey's movement, and regularly attended his meetings.[76]

Among the UNIA's several hundred branches, none was further from Harlem than Sydney. Even there, Garvey's program was taken up in 1924 in the creation of the Australian Aboriginal Progressive Association. 'The Australian Aboriginal Progressive Association', began a report in the *Negro World*, 'has blazed a trail for him, and he is following the trail. We do not think he will turn back. He has nothing to lose and everything to gain by pushing forward, whatever the obstacles he may encounter.'[77] The further Aboriginal people 'pushed forward', the closer they came to achieving self-sufficiency. To progress was to close in a gap created by having been dispossessed of their land and forced into a position of socio-economic deficit and disadvantage. Progress in this settler-colonialist context meant the extent to which activists stopped the removal of Aboriginal children from their families, gained equal citizenship, protected Aboriginal cultural identity and possessed the means to provide for themselves through land ownership. The categories (national citizenship, land ownership) were ones the British had brought with them, and the bearers of the world's oldest living culture had little choice but to measure themselves against them. Their experience from a position of relative disadvantage is instructive of the experiences of colonised subjects everywhere.

What futures, meanwhile, did colonial subjects see in their pasts? In India, the largest and most lucrative of Britain's possessions, the economic exploitation that the 'Grand Old Man of India' Dadabhai Naoroji described as the 'drain theory' intensified resentment of British rule and turned the attention of India's early nationalists to the example of Meiji Japan.[78] The Indian National Congress that eventually led India to Independence recommended in 1902 that the state take practical steps to encourage the revival and development of indigenous art, manufacturing and new industries. In this respect, the example

---

[76] Martin, *Marcus Garvey*, 65.

[77] *Negro World* (20 September 1924) quoted in Maynard, *Fight for Liberty and Freedom*, 33–4.

[78] Naoroji, *Poverty and Un-British Rule in India*.

of Japan's development of its native industries, in particular its silk production, was held up for emulation by Indian leaders.[79] The question that followed concerned what aspects of indigenous Indian art and culture were to be revived and developed. On what scale, spatial and temporal, were Indians to view their past in order to construct a model for the future?

Richard Weiss has studied an obscure Tamil poet for whom the scale was that of the local indigenous community and its ancient religious traditions.[80] At the margins of colonial cosmopolitanism, Ramalinga Swami took inspiration from Shaiva tradition and reformulated it in creative and even radical ways. Past tradition proved no impediment to future progress. From native religious categories he found the very means to break with the descent communities that dominated India and establish an elective society where aspirants navigated their way through past traditions, discarded those elements they regarded as superficial, and in so engaging with past traditions discovered their underlying truths. Ramalinga distinguished the truth of tradition, which he rejected, from the truth of taking one's own journey through them. By giving oneself over to tradition one gained the resources that were to be sifted through, redefined and revived. His teachings at the periphery of colonial activity advanced a critical and creative reformulation of home-grown religious categories, and his example suggests that an orientation towards tradition need not necessarily entail resistance to change, reform and innovation. The traditions changed as followers rediscovered them in the light of the present day.

In contrast to Ramalinga's revivalist traditionalism, China in the twentieth century offers the prime example of an iconoclastic society that saw no future in its past. Progress meant the full-scale obliteration of Chinese traditions. The May Fourth Movement (*Wu-ssu yün-tung*) marks the day in 1919 when 3,000 university students assembled in today's Tiananmen Square to denounce the Chinese government's humiliating acceptance of Japanese control over Shantung province, four years after Japan's notorious Twenty-One Demands had wounded the pride of the Chinese people by allowing Japan to establish itself as a colonial power in China. Rallying cries such as 'save the nation', 'don't forget the national humiliation', 'externally, resist the Great Powers' and 'internally, throw out the traitors', reflected the feeling of national humiliation, the belief that China's ills were a result of imperialism and the new-found determination to build a stronger China through intellectual and social reform.

The action needed to insure against future humiliations required the total destruction of everything old. Antiquity had until then provided Chinese culture

---

[79] Chandra, *Rise and Growth of Economic Nationalism in India*, 113–14.
[80] Weiss, *Emergence of Modern Hinduism*.

with its standard of excellence. Merchandise advertised as old-fashioned fetched the highest price, the most trusted medicines were those 'handed down from the ancestors' and the most venerated styles of literary expression, painting and calligraphy were those that followed the ancient models. The same applied to ethical principles, philosophy and political and economic theories.

The new Chinese were young Chinese. They were sufficiently uncorrupted by the traditions of the past and thus capable of destroying the old culture and building a new society. In their iconoclastic fervour, the new youth movement acted to dismantle age-old conventions and superstitions pervading Chinese society. They promoted Western ideas of science and democracy while fiercely attacking Chinese forms of ethics, literature, philosophy, history, religion and political institutions. Various forms of liberalism, pragmatism, utilitarianism, anarchism and socialism were Western and to be discussed earnestly. 'High school boys and girls listen soberly and intelligently to lectures on subjects that would create nothing but bored restlessness in an American school', observed the American philosopher and educational reformer John Dewey, clearly impressed by the vigour of the movement during a stay in China from 1919 to 1921. 'There is an eager thirst for ideas – beyond anything, I am convinced, in the youth of any other country on earth.'[81] These young Chinese dealt a devastating blow to Confucianism, accelerated the decline of the old family system and the rise of feminism, student and labour movements, the reorganisation of the Kuomintang, and the birth and ultimate victory in 1949 of the Chinese Communist Party.[82]

Dewey's two years in China took him to almost all the coastal provinces as well as several inland provinces where he mixed with Chinese people from all walks of life, professors, schoolteachers, students, officials, revolutionaries, warlords, gentry, merchants, and even peddlers and servants. He arrived as the first foreign scholar to be formally invited to China thanks to the efforts of a former Columbia University student of his, Hu Shih, the foremost political liberal in Republican China (1912–1949), a leader in establishing the vernacular as the official written language, and an advocate of mass education as a sounder means for social change than political revolution. Hu looked to Dewey as the expounder of a scientific method that could be applied to every aspect of human life and, more importantly, every problem of China's modernisation.[83] Progress was the cornerstone of the entire range of Dewey's thought. Every aspect of his philosophy – experience, intelligence, knowledge, logic, value, science,

---

[81] Dewey (1921) quoted in Chow, *May Fourth Movement*, 186.
[82] Chow, *May Fourth Movement*, 1–2, 19–23, 182–6. See further Wang, *Inventing China through History*.
[83] Wang, *John Dewey in China*.

education – derived its meaning from how it improved humankind's relationship with its environment. Dewey believed that if the experimental method in science and philosophy were systematically applied to the pressing social and political questions of the day, merely gratuitous social change might be converted into consciously constructed and directed social improvement.[84] Hu agreed and regarded Dewey's experimentalism as the most advanced stage in the progress of Western culture. His intellectual endeavour consisted in making Chinese culture a scientific culture in which everything was to be held to the standards of the Deweyan method.

A gentler version of change than that offered by the iconoclasts came from advocates of the adoption of Western science, technology and institutions who attempted to prove that they were upheld by the ancient sages, including Confucius. Conservatives opposed even to that offered a defence of tradition based on a nonprogressive account of time. Some argued that a historically developed national essence (*kuo ts'ui*) offered people a common identity that also underpinned their age-old social and political customs. Others turned to the idea of change itself to expose the folly of forcing particular changes, either by drawing upon the European concept of organic evolution, with its notion of the subordination of the individual to a transcendent historical wisdom, or by theorising a sequence of deterministic historical cycles leading humankind in a direction away from contemporary industrialism. The conservative positions revealed a deep influence of Taoist teachings of the cyclical and relative nature of temporal existence, and thus the futility of struggle against the rhythms of the cosmos. They were efforts by thinkers of a revolutionary age to arrive at a form of perennial conservativism – doctrines that tell us why the past as such is intrinsically valuable, and why its heritage must be protected by any person in any age or place.[85]

These examples from Japan, black America, indigenous Australia, India and China illustrate how different collectivities acted to tilt the weighing scale that is relative progress in their favour. The universalistic construction of absolute progress was the external standard against which relative advances were measured. During these decades in Britain, Europe and the United States, an ideology of social reform also sought to bring greater equilibrium to the sectors of society for whom industrialisation had delivered more losses than gains. New liberalism, not to be confused with the neoliberalism that came later, developed in Britain in the 1880s, led to a deluge of social reform in the period from 1906 to 1914 and laid the foundation for projects that in the interwar and postwar years authorised a greater degree of government intervention than that tolerated by

---

[84] Marcell, *Progress and Pragmatism*, 216, 247. [85] Furth, 'May Fourth in History', 65–6.

classical nineteenth-century liberalism, from Franklin D. Roosevelt's New Deal to John Maynard Keynes's ideas-leadership of postwar reconstruction. The belief in a free, self-regulating market, reflecting natural law and ensuring social justice, collapsed in the face of the realities unmasked by society's increasing awareness of socio-economic inequality. Introduced in the initial flurry of reform were old-age pensions, insurance against sickness and unemployment, school meals and medical services. Minimum wages were fixed in certain industries and attempts were made at income and wealth redistribution.[86]

New liberals believed collectivism was necessary because in the words of L. T. Hobhouse, one of their earliest and leading lights, 'it is a simple principle of applied ethics that responsibility should be commensurate with power'.[87] Since the state possessed the most power, it was the most responsible for securing the conditions for the common good. The prospects for social progress relied on an intelligent and activist-interventionist state capable of regulating the forces essential to the welfare of the community. The state in its activities exhibited the inner moral and spiritual interests of its members, and an idealist conception of progress (see section two) acted in the service of social reform by revealing the historical development of mind and thus the improving ethical framework of human society. The idealist doctrine that mind comes before matter saw the reformers place substantial store in education as the surest path for guiding society towards increasing social progress. By conceiving the community as an organisation of rationally and ethically cooperating individuals, they upheld the liberal belief in unimpeded individual improvement while advocating a collectivism of mutual responsibility and social solidarity. This was progress in the form of social legislation delivered to the groups of society identified as the most in need.

In Germany, the community that mattered was the *Volksgemeinschaft* or national community, at the core of which lay the 'ontological dilemma' of attempting to scientise an inherently organicist *Volk* concept historically linked to aesthetic notions of language, customs, spirit and myth.[88] The early Nazi years witnessed the rapid institutionalisation of '*völkisch* research', forced a resolution to this dilemma and ultimately bled the concept of its essential transcendental quality. State support for the institutions of national community waned and the 1936 Nazi Four-Year Plan redirected resources to science and engineering.

Rather than highlighting unevenness and incommensurability, relative progress might draw attention to the 'scale of forms', the constellation of related

---

[86] Hay, *Origins of the Liberal Welfare Reforms*, 11; Freeden, *New Liberalism*, 19.

[87] Hobhouse, *Liberalism*, 164. See further Freeden, *New Liberalism*, 66–70.

[88] Hare and Link, 'Idea of *Volk* and the Origins of *Völkisch* Research', 575–96.

terms that each embody the 'generic essence' of the idea of progress. There is
a sense in which the terms explored above to elucidate the category of relative
progress – tradition, revivalism, iconoclasm, reform – only underscore the
universality of the concept, for they each foreground a future to be created
based on an image of the past. Yet unlike the armchair historical philosophising
of absolute progress, relative progress required leaders capable not merely of
evoking the links between the past, present and future, but of forging them anew
in collective action. In the second half of the twentieth century, planners went
ahead in surmising that they had grasped the direction of history and in
constructing their collective projects on its tracks. Neoliberals, meanwhile,
switched scales, inveighed against collectivist designs and pooled their efforts
into dissociating progress from history, recasting the concept into the spontaneous and non-historical order of the free marketplace for every individual to
seize.

4 Everybody's Progress

Times of crisis call for radical re-imaginings of the present order. In the midst of
the destruction of the Second World War, reconstruction had already begun,
offering planners the opportunity to draft their visions for a better future.[89] In
a newly independent India, the emergent bipolar global order meant picking
sides, combining the best of the capitalist and communist systems or attempting
to remain neutral while steering one's own course. The legendary figure of
swaraj Mahatma Gandhi had worried that his friend and first Prime Minister of
India, Jawaharlal Nehru, would pursue a hybrid model. He wrote in 1940 that
'Nehru wants industrialization because he thinks that if it is socialized, it would
be free from the evils of capitalism. My own view is that the evils are inherent in
industrialism, and no amount of socialization can eradicate them.'[90]

Gandhi's concerns turned out to be vindicated. Nehru went full steam ahead
with creating a parliamentary regime that would run the affairs of a modern,
industrialised state, where labour and agrarian movements were subordinated to
top-down agendas of change through planned economic development, and
social reform through law and legislation. Gandhi's almost magical political
efficacy derived precisely from the fact that he tapped into and found peace in an
India that Nehru the arch-secularist wished to overhaul. Nehru's historical
investigations put India's past before the tribunal of modernity and found it
unfit for the task of the future. 'To live a self-sufficient village life cut off from
the rest of the world', his study of world history had taught him, 'was not

---

[89] See, for example, Macintyre, *Australia's Boldest Experiment*.
[90] Fischer, *Essential Gandhi*, 292.

conducive to progress in anything'.[91] A historian-politician attempting to forge an independent path for India, Nehru exemplifies several of the main threads of twentieth-century thinking on history and progress – history as a guide to politics, the loss of faith in historical progress and the subsequent belief in the state as an instiller of purposeful directionality in a world characterised by irrationality and unpredictability.

The product of Harrow and Cambridge, Nehru exuded the very essence of colonial cosmopolitanism. His historical writings reflected his dual heritage and passed through two principal phases, the first Marxist and the second liberal.[92] In *Glimpses of World History* (1934) and *The Discovery of India* (1946), Nehru emphasised the natural environments and laws of historical development that circumscribe human action, the elucidation of which Marx, in his view, offered the only scientific account. He followed Hegel in tracing the development of Spirit from East to West, but there in the Germanic lands it was not destined to repose. The First World War and its unparalleled devaluation of human life, together with the first signs of decolonisation, underscored the declining position of the West and gave reason to believe that Asia could reclaim the Spirit and its central place in world history. Western liberalism would always be subordinated to the interests of Western imperialism. It needed to be given new life in India and elsewhere.

The mid-century conjunction of war, India's bloody partition, independence, technological innovation and the advent of nuclear weaponry led Nehru to dispense with his Marxism. History conceived on the scale of the dialectic – a rational process governed by discernible laws – seemed fanciful in a world where scientific achievements were increasingly put to harmful ends. Irrationality was the more important category than rationality, and this exposed the unreliability of the past as a guide to political action. By 1958 there were 'new problems for which we have not got parallels or historical precedents elsewhere ... Science is advancing far beyond the comprehension of a very great part of the human race, and posing problems which most of us are incapable of understanding, much less solving.'[93] The new radically empowered agent of history backed by science and technology rendered the task of mediation between past and future vastly more difficult, perhaps impossible, and transformed the experience of the present into one of radical novelty and discontinuity. As Zoltán Simon has argued, the postwar historical sensibility was one that expected the future not to develop from previous states but to bring about 'something unprecedented'.[94] The new task of politics

---

[91] Nehru, *Glimpses of World History*, 422.
[92] Purushotham, 'World History in the Atomic Age', 837–67.
[93] Nehru (1958) quoted in Purushotham, 'World History in the Atomic Age', 845.
[94] Simon, *History in Times of Unprecedented Change*, 7.

consisted in mastering the machine in the interests of humankind without humankind in turn being transformed into a machine in the interests of the state, capital or other instrumentality. No law-bound historical process would do the work. The state had to bring about the conditions conducive to progress.

The global served Nehru as a temporal rather than a spatial category. History illuminated to him that political action takes place within a space of competing temporalities on which the past exerts influence and the future exerts demands. History formed the sovereign horizon of politics. It could not be transcended but was a kind of sphere of existence that 'operated on a global scale'.[95] Nehru's statism was animated by a desire to order time to create what François Hartog has termed a 'regime of historicity' that linked together the past, present and future of the Indian nation. The state needed not only to survive in time but to structure time itself. It achieved this through five-year plans, regularly scheduled elections and the regular operations of the developmental state. Measuring progress through statistics imposed a temporal framework on the life of the nation and instituted a comforting chronology of incremental movement in an age perceived to be defined by an accelerated and disorienting indeterminacy.

Most important to Nehru was fostering this sense of historical directionality. As he told the journalist Tibor Mende in 1955, 'once the people realize that you are going in a certain direction, they are optimistic. They are prepared to put up with delay, a little delay, because they know that they are going toward something. It is only when they feel that they are not going any way that they become angry.'[96] Nehru reasoned that an emphasis on the future as a 'horizon of expectation' could ease the heavy burden of India's past. A pillar of the Nehruvian state – centralised planning – signified not only a certain future later but also a more secure anchorage in the present now. Planning was as much about creating a space for thinking and action in the present as it was about the future gains to be enjoyed further down the road. It took care of the means as much as the ends.

India won its independence in the same year that an international thought collective, mostly economists with a sprinkling of historians and philosophers, gathered at the Swiss ski resort of Mont Pèlerin to establish the charter of a political program that would come to be known as neoliberalism. They were there at the invitation of F. A. Hayek, the Austrian economist and political philosopher, and they were united by their shared distrust of the authoritarian, if not despotic, tendencies of postwar planning and reconstruction, the kind of top-

---

[95] Purushotham, 'World History in the Atomic Age', 839–40.
[96] Mende, *Conversations with Mr. Nehru*, 48.

down instilling of historical directionality that we just saw in the example of
Nehru and the kind of collectivism and government interventionism that we
encountered earlier in the example of early twentieth-century new liberalism,
with its analogues in Marxist and British Fabian socialism, social democracy,
paternalist conservatism, the New Deal and the totalitarianisms of the left and
right. In Hayek's memorable phrase, these were all the 'road to serfdom'. Their
makers' pretentions 'to know the desirable direction of progress' were to him
'the extreme of hubris. Guided progress would not be progress.'[97] Instead, one
ought to create the policies most favourable to progress and then withdraw and
hope for the best. In evolutionary terms that were central to Hayek's thinking,
the projects by social reformers to alleviate poverty and inequality imposed an
artificial cooperative order on human societies that incline naturally to spon-
taneity and competition.[98] This led in the long run to blind acceptance of
government intervention and a deepening susceptibility to coercion and
totalitarianism.

   Here we are switching scales from progress conceived as a collective activity
to progress conceived as a task for every individual. Hayek's project to renew
classical liberalism did not completely reject collective planning, but it was
planning for competition rather than planning against competition.[99] Alongside
him in Switzerland, the American economist and hugely influential leader of
the Chicago school of economics, Milton Friedman, would specify their task
as one of minimising the state's ability to intervene in the activities of
individuals while simultaneously authorising the state to 'police the system',
to 'establish the conditions favourable to competition and prevent monopoly',
to 'provide a stable monetary framework, and relieve acute poverty and
distress ... neoliberalism proposes that it is competition that will lead the
way'.[100] Humankind's competitive passions were higher-grade fuel for
propelling society forward than the stolid dictates of those with visions of
the road ahead. Progress did not come with a guided tour but rather sprang
from the spontaneous orders or self-generating systems observable in
biological evolution and free-market competition.

   The term 'neoliberalism' is prone to overuse and in consequence difficult to
pin down. It can be invoked in the broadest sense to denote a form of market
fundamentalism and to characterise the host of attitudes and policies aimed at
deregulation, privatisation and individual self-sufficiency. It can also be invoked
pejoratively in protest moments opposing the global and local impositions of
this regulatory framework (deregulation itself is a regulatory framework).

---

[97] Hayek, *Law, Legislation and Liberty*, 169.
[98] Angner, 'History of Hayek's Theory of Cultural Evolution', 695–718.
[99] Hayek, *Road to Serfdom*, 43.   [100] Friedman, 'Neoliberalism and Its Prospects', 92.

Curiously, for a term that has become synonymous with Americanisation and the market-oriented doctrines of the so-called Washington consensus agencies, including the World Bank and International Monetary Fund, neoliberalism lacks purchase in the United States, where the word 'liberal' is associated with the left-interventionism most critics of neoliberalism tend to support.[101] It grew in fact from interwar German Ordoliberalism and the Colloque Walter Lippmann in Paris, but only from the summit of Mont Pèlerin were its petitions taken up across the Atlantic.

At the core of neoliberalism is the conviction that competition left to its own devices tends to more efficient norms, rules, codes and liberal institutions. Margaret Thatcher made no bones about the source of this conviction when she once interrupted a policy meeting brandishing Hayek's *Constitution of Liberty* while sternly declaring 'this is what we believe'.[102] As an enemy of historicism in the totalising and highly misleading version of it criticised by his friend Karl Popper, Hayek could only imply the universal validity of competition in an evolutionist order tending to greater efficiency. He was careful to note that it could only 'show how complex structures carry within themselves a means of correction that leads to further evolutionary developments'.[103] He could not explicitly argue that increasing efficiency was bound to occur in the passage of time, for that would be to subscribe to historicism or historical law.[104] By Popper's well-known and idiosyncratic account, historicism consisted in 'an approach to the social sciences which assumes that historical prediction is their principle aim, and which assumes that this aim is attainable by discovering the "rhythms" or the "patterns", the "laws" or the "trends" that underlie the evolution of history'.[105] Were these discernible, Hayek and Popper agreed, it would only take a dictator to accelerate the journey towards the final and happy destination, justifying anything to achieve the goal and disposing of whomever proved an obstacle.

Popper attended the meeting at Mont Pèlerin before withdrawing from the group on account of its refusal to admit socialists. Popper was no socialist himself, but his vision of an open society was one in which opposing views faced off in rational debate. His critical rationalism was at once a philosophy of science and a political philosophy. To qualify as knowledge, scientific theories and propositions had to pass the test of falsification – a single demonstration of evidence to the contrary eliminated a candidate from consideration. This model of critical experimentation in the *Logic of Scientific Discovery* (1934) then became the model for critical debate in the sphere of politics, that is, the

---

[101] Peck, *Constructions of Neoliberal Reason*, xi–2.   [102] Ranelagh, *Thatcher's People*, ix.
[103] Hayek, *Fatal Conceit*, 25.   [104] Traver, 'Hayek's View of History', 25–30.
[105] Popper, *Poverty of Historicism*, 3.

Open Society (1945). The task of politics consisted not in intuiting the direction of history and constructing plans for the future accordingly, but simply in treating individual problems on their individual merits, holding up each problem to the criteria of rational argumentation and proceeding piecemeal in this fashion.[106] An appropriate mix of contending viewpoints enabled arguments to be scrutinised, some discarded, some retained and most modified in the clash of ideas. Whatever progress ensued in the absence of such an arrangement would be the materialisation of a dogma.

We have examined progress alongside tradition, first in Indian revivalist traditionalism and then in twentieth-century Chinese iconoclasm. Now in the context of post-war liberalism, an exchange between Popper and the conservative English philosopher Michael Oakeshott points to the difficulty of leaving the past behind even in approaches focused exclusively on the present at hand. Progress to Popper was the aggregate sum of problems solved on a case-by-case basis. His conception lacked directionality and was essentially ahistorical in the manner of Hayekian spontaneous order. Oakeshott regarded politics as a conversation less about argument and problems requiring solutions than about protecting and preserving a way of life, tradition, or what he later called 'practice'.[107] As he penned in a letter to Popper in 1948, 'no problem in politics should be allowed to get out of proportion and to exclude the real business of politics, which is to keep the society as a whole, in all its arrangements, coherent and stable as well as progressive'.[108] Progress benefited the more historical traditions were foregrounded. Critical rationalism placed excessive emphasis on technical knowledge, leading Popper's philosophy in its political application to place undue stress on solving problems. Oakeshott took from history that the attempt to solve one problem too often unsettled the whole of society. We are reminded here of Collingwood's anecdote about the lakeside community whose development of a new and more efficient fishing technique brought with it the collapse of the community's cherished way of life.

Oakeshott's comments led Popper to reconsider his position on tradition. He answered with a 'Rational Theory of Tradition' that presented the scientific tradition as a first-order tradition of handed-down theories on which the attitude of critical inquiry had been imposed as a second-order tradition.[109] It was for the critical second-order tradition to scrutinise the first-order tradition handed down from history. Historical tradition was but another

---

[106] Popper, *Logic of Scientific Discovery*; Popper, *Open Society and Its Enemies*.

[107] Oakeshott, *Human Conduct*. See further Oakeshott, *Rationalism in Politics*, 5–42.

[108] Oakeshott, letter to Popper (28 January 1948), provided in Jacobs and Tregenza, 'Rationalism and Tradition', 21.

[109] Jacobs and Tregenza, 'Rationalism and Tradition', 13–14.

object for science to attempt to falsify. Oakeshott considered this fanciful. We are according to him too embedded in our traditions or what Wittgenstein called 'forms of life' to attain a position from which we could come face to face with them, articulate them and criticise them. Oakeshott doubted that a tradition such as liberalism could be given new life in foreign soil in the style suggested by Nehru. Traditions depended on the soil from which they grew and were not transposable to new environments.

It took until the late 1970s for neoliberalism to become a full-fledged political practice. To combat high unemployment, sluggish exports and inflation, governments across the capitalist world moved to increase competitiveness and economic activity by deregulating financial markets and industries. Tax cuts on wealthy individuals and large corporations were hailed by conservatives as keys to increasing productivity, state-owned enterprises in industries such as telecommunications and energy were privatised, and into the 1980s and 1990s trade and investment liberalisation, deregulation, privatisation and economic integration were policy mainstays, empowering investors, speculators and business owners over workers and unions. Simultaneously, advocates of public choice theory brought the logic of the free market to bear on noneconomic issues. Human agents were now economic agents whose rational expectations in the marketplace saw them optimise the movement of goods and raise efficiency. Few aspects of living fell outside the purview of the newly formed conceptualisation of 'the economy' as the self-sufficient sum total of monetary flows governing the relations between production, distribution and consumption within national boundaries.[110]

The politics of free markets and public choice paired well with what came to be termed the 'economic growth paradigm'. During the Second World War, Gross National Product (GNP) figures had become popular for setting production targets and gauging the productive capacities of adversaries. At the end of hostilities, rapid growth enabled governments to respond to the challenges of demobilisation by creating stable jobs for potentially volatile populations. Long-standing social and class-based tensions were approached as non-ideological and technical problems of production and efficiency. Economic growth trumped alternative socio-economic agendas such as balance, stability and redistribution, which may have generated priorities other than the expansion of productive capacity and mass-consumption.[111] The singlemindedness with which it was pursued has led the environmental historian John McNeill to argue that 'economic growth was easily the most

---

[110] Macekura, *Mismeasure of Progress*, 169–71; Schmelzer, *Hegemony of Growth*, 13; Karabell, *Leading Indicators*, 73–90.
[111] Macekura, *Mismeasure of Progress*, 36–7.

important idea of the twentieth century'. Even the Cold War between the United States and the Soviet Union could be summed up as an attempt to outgrow the enemy. It was less a competition over which system was able to provide more equality, employment and democratic participation than which system was able to generate more material output domestically and abroad (Net Material Product in the Soviet bloc). The Organisation for Economic Cooperation and Development (OECD), the international organisation most dedicated to the objective of economic growth, has observed with a degree of self-criticism that throughout the twentieth century 'there was an implicit assumption that economic growth was synonymous with progress: an assumption that a growing GDP meant life must be getting better'.[112] Indeed, few marriages have fared so well as the one between growth and progress.

The growth paradigm emerged towards the end of the 'trente glorieuses', the recent and small-scale history of the three decades from 1946 to 1975, during which national economies, in particular those of continental western Europe, achieved growth rates roughly triple the size of those experienced in the lengthy timeframe following industrialisation. This is the period that has subsequently been named the 'Great Acceleration' to describe the processes of accelerated change in earth system trends such as water usage, large dams, transportation, international tourism, fertiliser consumption, carbon dioxide emissions, ocean acidification and biosphere degradation – in short, the affluent society behind the ecological upheaval of our times.[113] Critics of growth came out in numbers in the 1970s to denounce the metrics of assessing progress and to propose alternative definitions of social value that prioritised concerns such as poverty reduction, environmental sustainability and social equality. The Indian economist Amartya Sen criticised an aggregate figure that 'is supremely unconcerned with the inter-personal distribution of that sum. This should make it a particularly unsuitable approach to use for measuring or judging inequality.' In the outpouring of social and ecological critique, Fred Hirsch argued influentially that the promise of economic growth pervading society had reached an impasse. It was no longer credible to assume that increasing material wealth delivers social benefits. What the proponents of economic growth overlooked was that as societies become wealthier, an increasing proportion of goods and services become unavailable to everyone. Material affluence did not make for a better society. The affluent society was in fact the frustrated society, amassing its wealth while seeing no improvement in the overall condition of every one of its members.[114]

---

[112] McNeill, *Something New under the Sun*, 236; OECD, *Statistics, Knowledge and Policy*, back cover.

[113] Fourastié, *Les Trente glorieuses*; Schmelzer, *Hegemony of Growth*, 14.

[114] Sen, *Economic Inequality*, 16; Hirsch, *Social Limits to Growth*; Arndt, *Rise and Fall of Economic Growth*.

We may appear to have digressed into matters of twentieth-century political economy. This is not so. The point being developed here is an important one and will carry into our final section. It concerns the manner in which the measurement of economic growth supplied a *narrative structure* for plotting the advance of nations from past to present and into the future. Gunnar Myrdal, the economist, sociologist and mind behind the establishment of the Swedish welfare state (*Folkhemmet*), expressed a reluctance to publish figures on per capita national income drawn from a two-year study of countries in Asia. 'That these figures have any precise meaning at all is doubtful', he wrote of his findings. A pioneer of the use of GNP, the British-Australian economist and statistician Colin Clark recognised the difficulty of deploying statistics in ways that were honest and meaningful. The 'growthmanship' that had come to dominate political discourse and policy described 'an excessive preoccupation with economic growth, advocacy of unduly simple proposals for obtaining it, and the careful choice of statistics to prove that countries with a political and economic system which you favour have made exceptionally good growth, and that the countries administered by your political opponents have made exceptionally poor economic growth'.[115] In the language of Hayden White, progress as economic growth emplotted numbers much as historical narratives emplotted facts.

'Statistics *are* a form of storytelling; quantitative evidence *needs* qualitative expressions of moral purpose to gain wide purchase … We value what we measure, and we measure what we value.' Stephan Macekura has stressed these points while arguing that economic growth became the dominant historical narrative in the twentieth century orienting governments and citizens to the relations between the past, present and future. Economic growth was an all-encompassing historical narrative, a 'description of the past', 'metanarrative for describing human civilisation' and 'metonym for human progress'.[116]

The new and compelling stories of growth offered by economists portrayed nation states as singular and homogenous entities, in contrast to the data presented by other social scientists that directed attention to questions of inequality between different social groups within nation states. The discipline of economics supplied the powerful statistical narratives that governments and citizens alike used to plot the development of the nation through time – the small-scale triumphant history of recent decades and the even more prosperous future to be won in the years to come. The recent history of economic performance assumed a preeminent position in public affairs and continues to this day to

---

[115] Myrdal, *Asian Drama*, 474; Clark, *Growthmanship*, 12–13.

[116] Macekura, *Mismeasure of Progress*, 9–10, 198.

define what leaders can and should do. As Morten Jerven has noted, the word statistics is directly linked to the word state and refers to the data that states collect to obtain knowledge of their internal economic and social conditions. The validity of economic statistics can thus be regarded as varying according to the power and legitimacy of the state or agency acting on its behalf. In the case of African economic development, Jerven's research has exposed the 'poor numbers' behind the repeatedly unsuccessful development programs of international financial agencies such as the World Bank.[117]

Comparison is another way that statistics can tell stories and create a sense of moral purpose. As the discipline of economics became more globalised, so its procedures became more standardised, and macroeconomic statistics or what David Speich has called 'global abstractions' emerged as a comparative framework that painted a picture of the world as a wretchedly poor place.[118] Viewed on a global and comparative scale, the enormous poverty of huge parts of the world became an analytic problem to be solved in its own right, no longer concealed in problems of colonial exploitation and exchange. The globalised space of macroeconomic quantification reflected the assumption that economic activity operates according to the same universal principles. It seemed possible to erase global poverty by formalising the secret of Western economic success and applying the solution in a limited set of policy recommendations to all economies across the globe. Macroeconomic statistics reduced the complexity of the human world, replaced multiplicities with aggregates, and were implemented as development models in countries that emerged as sovereign agents on the international stage in the wake of decolonisation.

As universal history made possible a conception of absolute progress, so the spontaneous and nonhistorical workings of the global marketplace, distilled in figures conveyed as a moral language, made possible a conception of everybody's progress.

5 Anti-progress

We began with conceptions of history that precluded the possibility of belief in progress. Now, with much of the world's attention on rising temperatures, mass extinction and environmental transformation, it is not so much that we cannot believe in progress, but rather that many have chosen to reject the idea. Although anti-progressivist pessimism is by no means new, there seems little doubt that we have in Thomas Moynihan's words become 'progressively conversant with progressively distal perils', accomplished readers of a future

---

[117] Jerven, *Poor Numbers*, 3.   [118] Speich, 'Use of Global Abstractions', 7–28.

that is bleak.[119] One may rebuff the notion that society has moved in a desirable direction and, on that basis, the expectation of future desirable gains. It may no longer make sense even to speak of such a link between historical understanding and future expectation, so little do the novelties of present-day experience conform to historical precedents. Zoltán Simon believes that we are today increasingly unable to understand this novel present as being part of a developmental process, and so the only present and future to speak of are ones of 'unprecedented change', requiring new concepts and methods different from those with which historians have traditionally explained developmental change.[120] In this new historical condition, human beings are not the purposeful makers of history they used to be. History might rather confirm Tolstoy's view that it is a haphazard catalogue of unintended consequences.

What stands out from the past two decades is that history has been supersized. Big history, deep history and the new geological periodisation of the Anthropocene have cast human beings in a new light and brought into question principles of historical practice long central to the self-identity of the discipline. Not only has time been expanded, it has also been diversified in multiple temporalities, challenging traditional notions of historical time and in particular the linear past, present and future order of historical sense-making. Helge Jordheim and Einar Wigen have argued that the concept of crisis may be outperforming progress as the chief collective singular doing the conceptual work of synchronising the 'multiple times' of the international order. As progress came of age when fields of human endeavour previously regarded as autonomous began to be viewed as united in a common forward-moving quest, so crisis draws together different meanings from different fields and practices, aggregates them in the one conceptual form and ultimately homogenises the globe's inherently diverse speeds and rhythms. Walter Benjamin would have seen little reason to choose between the two. 'The concept of progress', he once wrote, 'should be grounded in the idea of catastrophe. That things "just keep on going" *is* the catastrophe.'[121]

The turn to larger timescales cannot be separated from the view that our traditional historical methods are unable to grasp the full measure of past and present earth system change. Among historians, Dipesh Chakrabarty has been the leading voice behind the new periodisation of the Anthropocene, initially declared in the early 2000s by the Nobel-prize-winning atmospheric chemist Paul Crutzen as the idea that we live an age defined by human influence on the planet. In Chakrabarty's hugely influential language, this turns on the notion

---

[119] Moynihan, 'Existential Risk and Human Extinction', 1.

[120] Simon, *History in Times of Unprecedented Change*.

[121] Jordheim and Wigen, 'Conceptual Synchronisation', 424–5; Smith, *Benjamin*, 64.

that human beings have become 'geological agents'.[122] The main challenge posed to history by the Anthropocene is the problem of understanding human agency on both biological and planetary timescales. In fact, the Anthropocene could be said to spread us over three temporalities: the history of the earth system; the history of human life on the planet; and the more recent history of industrial civilisation or capitalism.[123]

In this predicament, it is no wonder that matters of scale have been of primary concern. Indeed the word scale features no less than forty times in Chakrabarty's 2018 article 'Anthropocene Time'. The Anthropocene draws attention to 'the sheer scale of human impact on the planet', and the current challenge consists in finding ways to reconcile the small scale of human history with the large geological scale of the planet. What 'seems "slow" in human and world-historical terms', according to Chakrabarty, 'may indeed be "instantaneous" on the scale of Earth history', but to make a difference politically we must resist thinking of the kind that 'leaves us feeling "out-scaled"'.[124] To regard human beings as geological agents is to upscale the temporal category of the human, but it also obliges us to downscale the existential category of the human in comparison with nonhuman agencies. History becomes the conjunction of – and indeed a process of codeswitching between – viewing ourselves in the smallness of planetary time, recognising our powerful effects on the earth, and all the while not losing sight of our historical and political agency.

No less has an attention to scale been at the heart of the establishment of 'big history', an approach to studying the past over a period of thirteen-thousand years that after gaining the support of Bill Gates's philanthropy began being rolled out in American high schools in 2011. David Christian, the historian behind the project, believes the expanded timespan can help to re-endow the study of history with a meaning that was lost when professionalisation broke up the discipline into narrow specialisms. To the question 'what is the scale on which history should be studied?' Christian took the founding of the *Journal of World History* in 1991 as an opportunity to argue that the enlargement of the spatial scale should be accompanied by an enlargement of the temporal scale. With such a move, history could play as important a role in modern industrial societies as 'traditional creation myths' played in nonindustrial societies, opening up the past to questions as profound as those posed in traditional creation myths. This re-endowment of meaning required historians to dispense with the view that 'largescale history means sacrificing detail and retreating to empty

---

[122] Chakrabarty, 'Climate of History', 206–7.
[123] Chakrabarty, *Climate of History in a Planetary Age*, 49.
[124] Chakrabarty, 'Anthropocene Time', 8, 30.

generalities' as well as with the view that 'at the large scale there is simply too much information for the historian to handle'.[125]

Christian proceeded to predict that 'over the next fifty years we will see a return of the ancient tradition of "universal history" ... global in its practice and scientific in its spirit and methods'. Universal history meant the 'attempt to understand history at all possible scales', blurring the boundaries between the human and natural sciences 'as history rediscovers an interest in deep, even law-like patterns of change'. The shift back to universal history will 'reveal a profound orderliness in human history', for only at the scale of many millennia do the 'pixels of human action generate clear patterns, and an awareness of these patterns will inevitably change how we think about history at smaller scales'.[126] Unlike Anthropocene time, big history does not trouble itself with the problem of having to straddle different and incompatible timescales, that is, how the identification of large patterns stretching over millennia could be relevant to the 'big questions' asked by human beings who live over a series of mere decades. It is taken for granted that discovering the large and lawlike patterns of change is a valuable existential antidote to the historicist slimness of imagination. Given this preference for the kind of universal history practised before the nineteenth century, it is no surprise that first on the list of adversaries are certain philosophical founders of history's disciplinary identity – Vico, Dilthey, Collingwood, Croce, the neo-Kantians – those who asserted the disciplinary autonomy of history by distinguishing its individualising procedures and forms of knowledge from those of the natural sciences that attempt to construct general and universally valid theories and systems. Perhaps the long-awaited truce has finally been reached between *Geisteswissenschaften* and *Naturwissenschaften*.

I take Chakrabarty and Christian to be representative of the new expanded scale that identifies a common foe in the importance traditionally assigned in the theory and practice of history to questions of human agency or the expression of human purpose. We should recall here a condition necessary for belief in progress, the one concerning *human action* being the vehicle moving humanity in its desired direction. We should also recall that we spent considerable time in section one distinguishing those conceptions of history that engender contemplative inaction from those that delight in the ability of human beings to act purposefully upon the world. In taking the challenge to Vico's idea that history is the study of what human beings have made with their own hands, the new ethos appears doubtful of the notion that human beings are the agents

---

[125] Christian, 'Case for "Big History"', 225, 227.

[126] Christian, 'Return of Universal History', 6–7, 20–1.

purposefully navigating a wise way forward. We should kiss goodbye history as the study of human desires, goals, purposes and intentions, and along with it the categories of freedom and necessity that have rooted the study of human actions in their distinct historical contexts. The fine texture of historical context cannot in any case be made out from the new vertiginous vantage point of historical reflection.

If not purposeful action, then what kind of agency is at work in the Anthropocene? Here the hugely influential notion of a 'technosphere', as developed by the geologist Peter Haff, provides the clearest picture. Haff attempts to solve the riddle of human agency in the Anthropocene, first, by distinguishing a 'geological Anthropocene' from a 'social Anthropocene'.[127] The former is the Anthropocene of earth system science and the efforts since 2009 to have it formally recognised in the earth's geological record. Concerned with identifying the markers in the earth's crust where human impact becomes visible, the evidence needed to make this determination has been sourced from the usual cause-effect explanations common to the natural sciences. The social Anthropocene, on the other hand, is the construction of humanities and social science scholars who for all their diversity of questions, concerns and approaches, have tended to use it as a framework for reconceptualising the place of human beings in the world. In the social Anthropocene, purposeful human action has retained its traditional explanatory role; indeed, much of the debate has concerned questions of periodisation that are in essence debates about the effects of different forms of human organisation – whether the features distinct to the period of human influence on the earth are germane to capitalism (Capitalocene), global economics (Econocene), the transatlantic mixing of the world's biota (Homogenocene), the establishment and mainten-ance of plantations (Plantationocene) or the disproportionate contributions of Great Britain and the United States to global carbon emissions since the Industrial Revolution (Anglocene). The social Anthropocene engages the con-ditions, motivations and histories of the world's peoples, including the role of politics, creativity and individual and collective agency.

Haff regards the separation as robbing the Anthropocene of its full explana-tory potential. The geological Anthropocene overlooks the fact that human beings are as much a product of the earth as the rocks they study, and at the other end of the spectrum the social Anthropocene neglects to consider the determining effects of the natural environment. The technosphere fuses the two versions in a view of the Anthropocene as a global network of humanmade technologies that in their total sum constitute an autonomous system whose

---

[127] Haff, 'Technosphere and Its Relation to the Anthropocene', 138.

internal dynamics constrain the behaviour of human beings. Like the other spheres – atmosphere, hydrosphere, lithosphere and biosphere – the technologies that crisscross the globe operate as an independent entity endowed with its own intrinsic purposefulness. 'In emerging as a global phenomenon', writes Haff, 'the technosphere has joined the classical spheres to become an autonomous Earth system, operating without direct human control ... the technosphere has agency, and that agency is not the same as our own'.[128] The consequence is devastating for humanistic notions of self-determination. Since we are dependent on the technosphere (it is estimated that without the support structure and services provided by technology the world's population would quickly shrink to its Stone Age base of roughly ten million individuals), what we like to think are freely taken actions are rather actions in support of the technosphere. The technosphere usurps individual human agency by incentives towards actions that ensure its survival. Even a mass movement to curtail global warming would require energy, materials, information and transportation in quantities that only the technosphere could supply at the required scale. Efforts to alter the future direction of humanity would only seal the current course.

It is no surprise, then, that the Anthropocene has been considered a threat to long-cherished notions of political agency. Madelaine Fagan suggests that we remain cautious of attempts to connect geological temporality with political temporality. Angela Last raises concern over the 'mournful focus on geology, in which humans seem to be automatically interred, geophysically active but politically passive'. The worry is that we could enter into a 'non-politics' of the Anthropocene, a 'post-politicisation' that occurs when politics is reduced to the sphere of consensual governing and policy making. Erik Swyngedouw fears that the challenges facing society could come to be seen as mostly managerial and technical problems, eliminating the space for disagreement and creativity by operating within a given political framework that remains beyond dispute. Similarly, when the political challenge of the Anthropocene is conceived as the problem of navigating the transition from one geological epoch to the next, Julia Nordblad points out that this closes down discussion of exactly what kind of futures are desirable and creatable.[129] If future political movements are to be movements in a desirable direction, they must preserve a conception of the future as essentially open and constructible by individual and collective decision making. We recall from section two the importance to the idea of progress of this constructability of the future by human action.

---

[128] Haff, 'Technosphere and Its Relation to the Anthropocene', 139, 143.

[129] Fagan, 'Dangers of an Anthropocene Epoch', 55; Last, 'We Are the World?' 163; Swyngedouw, 'Non-Political Politics of Climate Change', 5; Nordblad, 'Difference between Anthropocene and Climate Change Temporalities', 335.

If political agency is the exercise of purposeful action, then it has also been a long-cherished notion of humanistically oriented historiography. The category of 'the human' has come under attack in the Anthropocene as an unacceptable expression of human exceptionalism, a view of humankind as occupying a privileged position distinct from and superior to the rest of nature, and scholars working within its interdisciplinary framework have turned to constructions of human/nature entanglement and the so-called more than human. The philosopher of history Giuseppina D'Oro has identified strong and weak versions of the Anthropocene that approach the problem of human exceptionalism in terms of a distinction between the historical past and the natural past. Against the view that the historical past is human-centric, she has attempted to clarify that its subject matter is not human beings understood as a biological species whose temporalities are radically out of sync with the temporality of the planet. Rather, the subject matter of the historical past is the norms that govern human agents within fields of possibility and limitation, and never by reference to natural laws. What defines the historical past is a humanistic methodology, not an exclusive attention to humans. It is not an insignificant portion of planetary time because it is not a unit of time at all. Humanistically oriented historiography expresses a methodological commitment to examining the dynamic interplay of freedom and necessity, agency and structure, or simply the ways in which human beings have changed their conditions while also being shaped by them.[130]

The call by theorists of the Anthropocene for a 'negative universal history' may cheer the humanistically minded. At first glance, the idea of universal history appears entirely at odds with the ethos of the Anthropocene. First among the reasons why is that universal history as practised during the Enlightenment assumed the universality of natural law and expected to find in the human past patterns and regularities similar to those observed by natural scientists in nature, whereas the Anthropocene emphasises entanglement and diversity, and resists dualistic thinking. Second, universal history and its theory of absolute progress were highly optimistic regarding the future of humanity, whereas the Anthropocene is emblematic of a present-day pessimism whose focal point is extinction rather than abundance. And whereas universal history followed the scent of a collective actor – humankind, *Weltgeist*, proletariat – studies in the Anthropocene are in general conscious that some groups more than others have contributed to the warming of the planet. Universal history appears in league with the very mentality that the new ethos of the Anthropocene opposes.[131]

---

[130] D'Oro, 'In Defence of a Humanistically Oriented Historiography', 216–36.
[131] For a review of the conflict, see Boscov-Ellen, 'Whose Universalism?'

Harriet Johnson has argued by contrast that the Anthropocene itself is a universal insofar as it conceives 'history on a planetary scale' and presents humankind with the collective task of ensuring the conditions for its survival. Faced with this necessity, the historical imagination must be 'scaled up' if it is to explore the vastly expanded timescales unlocked by natural scientists, sometimes millions of years old, through which previously undetected global patterns of consumption and production, flourishing and extinction, enter into view (Johnson mentions the paleoclimatologists who take ice core samples of ancient air roughly 2.7 million years old). Since these patterns tend to reveal 'inequitable social relations', Johnson believes that the Anthropocene need not mean the end of aspirational agendas in the humanities and social sciences. The new periodisation may have dashed 'the old confidence that history unfolds with a plan for the better', but it can just as well inspire new critique and activism.[132] Yet we are left wondering what kind of political programs could possibly be raised from the identification of inequitable social relations millions of years old, in societies that even if they were to share certain of our present-day norms, operated within none of the institutional frameworks that characterise modern democratic society. Regrettably, history appears to disengage itself from the civic task of understanding public affairs, policy and institutions.

The more important issue seems to concern the nature of the collective actor that ultimately must move universal history. Chakrabarty points to 'a figure of the universal' that belongs to the grand sweep of history but avoids being engulfed by it. That figure is Adorno's negative universal, an approach to history that allows particulars to express their resistance to the general course of history without being denied their place in it. 'It remains true', wrote Adorno, 'that historical particulars are constantly the victims of the general course of history'. But they need not be. Rather than a universal history that presents a smoothed over collective actor unencumbered by the clutter of particulars, the Anthropocene demands a negative universal history in which the particulars at the margins of history constitute their own totality sweeping the globe precisely in their uneven and local manifestations. This is history for disillusioned times, for the individual elements that elude the general course of history, in Adorno's words, 'begin themselves to take on something of a contaminated, doom-laden aspect'.[133] What we are offered is a history of catastrophe methodology curiously combined with a positive political outlook.

For all the warranted attention to enlarged timescales, we should not be misled into thinking that they now constitute the bulk of historical research.

---

[132] Johnson, 'Anthropocene as a Negative Universal History', 48–53.

[133] Chakrabarty, *Climate of History in a Planetary Age*, 45; Adorno, '"Negative" Universal History', 95–6.

Indeed, the topics that animate discussion in the theory and philosophy of history do not necessarily echo in the corridors of university history departments. In response to Jo Guldi and David Armitage's suggestion that historians have only recently recovered an appropriately large perspective after a prolonged bout of myopic short-termism, Deborah Cohen and Peter Mandler have provided a reminder that much superb history continues to be conducted on timescales of several years to several decades and, moreover, that this ability to 'speak to multiple audiences on all the scales in which humans feel and think' is what has made the discipline 'an indispensable part of the educational and cultural landscape over the past generation'. When it comes to critiquing the idea of progress, some of the most convincing work has been conducted not on large timescales but rather according to long-standing historicist principles of unearthing the fine grain of historical context. Stephen Macekura has referred to the 'growth historicists' who have 'adopted a historicist perspective that treats economic growth *as* history, not an ahistorical term to describe a metanarrative of material progress'. They have, in other words, alerted us to the probability that the kind of growth experienced in the past *belongs to the past*. It will not necessarily be experienced in the current century, for 'the growth paradigm is neither universal nor natural'.[134] History studied on a scale of several decades reveals that growth was a contingent historical phenomenon that arose from distinct sociotechnical circumstances.

We saw in the previous section that the measurement of economic growth supplied a narrative structure for plotting the advance of nations through past, present and future. Among the growth historicists, Robert Gordon's study of the rise and fall of American growth is exemplary of the efforts to revise these narratives of growth as the dominant story of the twentieth century. Gordon's thesis is that some inventions matter more than others and that, in consequence, 'progress occurs much more rapidly at some times than others'. He terms the period from 1870 to 1970 the 'special century' that thanks to a 'unique clustering of Great Inventions' led to a 'singular interval of rapid growth' that we should not expect to see repeated. Growth in the United States slowed down from 1970 not due to a lack of new inventions or entrepreneurial vigour, but because the fundamental elements of the modern standard of living had by then already been achieved along so many varied dimensions, including food, housing, transportation, entertainment, communication, health and working conditions. The story since then has been a 'narrower palette of progress' combined with diminishing returns. Whereas the major innovations of the

---

[134] Cohen and Mandler, '*History Manifesto*: A Critique', 542; Macekura, *Mismeasure of Progress*, 198–9, 207.

special century altered almost every aspect of life (think for example of the abundantly diverse applications of electricity), the innovations of the past few decades in information technology and communications have been 'relevant only to a limited sphere of human experience'. As for social progress, income stagnation for the bottom ninety percent of earners could suggest that 'there has been no progress at all'.[135]

Gordon's stance regarding future progress clashes with that of 'techno-optimists' and highlights the manner in which claims about progress are claims to historical knowledge. 'No one can foresee the future', writes Gordon, 'but we can ask whether the future is more likely to resemble the dot-com decade of 1994–2004 or the more recent decade, 2004–14'.[136] His answer is that future growth will resemble the slow pace of the more recent period, not the faster growth of 1994–2004, much less the even more momentous growth of the period from 1920 to 1970. By Gordon's analysis, the principal benefits of the growth achieved by the digital revolution were concentrated in the decade 1994–2004. The following decade witnessed diminishing returns from new innovations, and from that data he predicts a future of much of the same.

The techno-optimists, on the other hand, extrapolate from the high-performing 1990s and downplay the poorer outcomes of more recent times. Erik Brynjolfsson and Andrew McAfee believe that we are 'at an inflection point' between a past of slow technological change and a future of breakneck transformation. The 'second machine age' will be that in which computers and other digital technologies provide at ever-higher levels the mental power that has been as important to progress as physical power.[137] But with this optimism comes pessimism. The more the future is cast as one of machines rapidly replacing humans, the more we should expect job destruction and mass unemployment. Against this techno-optimistic pessimism, Gordon's techno-pessimism depicts a rosier future where slower technological change on the rates of recent years sees news jobs created as rapidly as technology destroys old jobs. The two visions of the future differ precisely in the way they extrapolate from two different sets of historical information.

Ecomodernism is a variety of techno-optimism that returns us to the large scale of the Anthropocene and the ecomodernist view that the planet earth has been made by human hands and can continue to be remade by human hands. Ecomodernists stand opposed to the argument that continued population growth and economic expansion will outstrip the capacity of human beings to feed themselves and provide themselves with the necessary material resources.

---

[135] Gordon, *Rise and Fall of American Growth*, 2–3, 7–8, 605, 641.
[136] Gordon, *Rise and Fall of American Growth*, 602.
[137] Brynjolfsson and McAfee, *Second Machine Age*, 8–9.

Theirs is the neoclassical argument that innovation will continue to enable the substitution of newer, cleaner technologies for older, dirtier technologies, and thereby avert environmental catastrophe. Similarly, an impressive selection of philosophers, social scientists and business leaders have gathered together since 2013 in the Society for Progress to think through ways of achieving progress while enriching it with insights from moral and social philosophy.[138]

Advocates of the idea of 'degrowth', translated in the early 2000s from the French *décroissance*, might suggest that an alternative to progress is to be found in their efforts to radically reorganise politics and economics along the lines of their founder Serge Latouche's 8-R-program – reconceptualising, re-evaluating, restructuring, redistributing, relocalising, reducing, reusing, recycling.[139] Degrowth brings together a diverse group of scholars and activists under the common objective of opposing growth in all its forms, including 'green growth', which they see as buying into the comfortable illusion that techno-economic adjustments and ecomodernist innovations will allow humanity to continue its journey down the path of endless progress, only this time in harmony with the environment. To them, it is a matter of growth with environ-mental consequences or learning to prosper without growth.[140] As a historical orientation, the degrowth proposition that human beings can flourish in situations of material scarcity beckons the historical imagination to journey to regions of the past where this may have been so. History conducted on all the scales that human beings have experienced and made sense of the world might play a central role in this project of illuminating the full diversity of possibilities for human flourishing.

---

[138] ecomodernism.org; societyforprogress.org.   [139] Muraca, 'Décroissance', 159.

[140] Jackson, *Prosperity without Growth*. See the arguments for and against green growth in Dale et al., *Green Growth*.

Epilogue

Over the past few decades, usage of the word progress has been in decline while usage of the word crisis has been on the rise. Crisis seems to correspond to a reality that progress does not. The idea of progress remains today largely associated with the category of *absolute progress*, the one-size-fits-all model that lost its lustre the moment it became apparent that the concept contained components that were not working together in perfect harmony after all. The collective singular broke apart and exposed the fundamental disparities that made it the task of every group to achieve its own version of *relative progress*.

Concerned as I have been with Vico's humanistic notion of history as made by human hands, the emerging concept of crisis may prove effective in foregrounding both the present and past presents as sites of purposeful human action, contexts of indeterminacy and possibility, where events are eventful because they could have gone differently. A crisis calls for action, the delay of which would be disastrous. The concept might thus serve as an antidote to the inactive complacency long viewed as inherent to the idea of progress. With this comes the danger, of course, that crisis is deployed to legitimise the furtherance of present-day priorities, narrowing research agendas and disincentivising free and independent inquiry. There are even times when the theory and philosophy of history appears headed in the direction of so-called future studies, so much has the scientific community in general been swept up by the multiple crises that are now one big crisis, by what Gabriele Gramelsberger has diagnosed as a shift towards the 'future perfect mode' and by the notion that historical understanding is fundamental to what Riel Miller has termed 'futures literacy'.[141]

Crisis talk may be drowning out progress talk, but we have far from left the idea of progress behind. It retains a powerful authority that continues to structure our historical, political, scientific and moral imaginations. Barack Obama and Olaf Scholz are examples of leaders who have used the word to conjure up a lost sense of collective purpose. In popular science, the view that progress is the collective sum of advances made in different mainly technical fields remains powerfully pervasive. Patrick Collison and Tyler Cowan spoke for it in 2019 when they called for the inauguration of a new discipline of 'Progress Studies'.[142] The new discipline would identify the mechanics of

---

[141] Gramelsberger, 'From Science to Computational Sciences', 20; Miller, 'Futures Literacy'. On the future in present-day theory and philosophy of history, see Simon and Deile, *Historical Understanding*, 119–97, as well as the Historical Futures series of *History and Theory*.

[142] Collison and Cowen, 'We Need a New Science of Progress'.

progress in a full array of fields and in its collective output supply a blueprint for overall progress. They were partly right to point out that each discipline is already engaged in its own version of progress studies, for each discipline operates according to norms and principles that endow recent findings with a greater value than older findings (even though I have insisted on calling this developmental improvement). The first priority as they see it consists in bringing to an end this specialisation and fragmentation. Progress Studies would restore the cooperative impulse of *absolute progress*, smooth over the nuisance inconsistencies of *relative progress* and imbue with new élan the efficiency, productivity and innovation ambitions of *everybody's progress*.

Progress Studies was duly mocked by historians. History, they pointed out, has long taken care of accounting for the factors behind human successes and failures. Most unacceptably, Progress Studies would mean dispensing with the lesson that there are no direct lessons from the past. There is something deeply vulgar to historians in the idea that insights from the past can be applied to present-day circumstances, as if their efforts to illuminate the context-dependency of human behaviour amounted to nothing. But it might be that I am speaking of a certain kind of historian, or one who is on the way out. A thrust behind the new enlarged scales of historical reflection is an attempt to recalibrate temporal coordinates in ways that would authorise previously prohibited shifts between past, present and future modes. Understanding was the goal of the old variety of historian. The new variety, hope Collison and Cowen, might take up the task of diagnosing and treating.

The proposal received the ridicule it deserved. It offered a crude account of the past as serving the present and it indulged a naïve confidence in science being the welcomed mistress of every home. But for all the justified derision, there was something disconcerting in the attitudes expressed by the historical community towards the idea of progress. It was one of a number of occasions during the completion of this project that I became acutely aware that I was giving my time to an enormously unfashionable concept. Under the heading of progress grew a list of contemporary undesirables. Progress, it seemed, was complicit with the evils of historical time, chronology, linearity and periodisation. The idea of progress was at once the ideology of progress, and any notion of goal-directed action could be dismissed as teleological (an overused and increasingly misused term in historical parlance). I distinguished progress from developmental improvement and defended the value of thinking carefully about the idea against those with more radical and iconoclastic aspirations.

I was sympathetic to the claim that no amount of attention to non-Western perspectives could compensate for the fact that my conceptual framework derived from European modernity. Judged by these standards, other cultures were inevitably to deviate and be deprived of tendering alternatives to the dominant conception. The same could be said of premodern societies. The long expanse of time from antiquity to modernity may have failed to satisfy the conditions necessary for belief in progress, but that is because they are modern criteria, and the failure to satisfy them does not mean that premodern minds did not contemplate the nature of betterment in time.

My sense is that this worry is misdirected, chiefly because there are more appropriate names than progress for the various alternatives. Improvement is an important aspect of progress, but it is only one among numerous aspects. As I have tried to show, progress is a philosophy of history that presupposes specific relations between the past, present and future. It was a temporal orientation that governed ideas about human purpose in intellectual conditions specific to time and place, which went on to be accepted, rejected, modified and reconceived. A puzzling feature of the contemporary tendency to condemn progress is that it is often articulated alongside hopes that the idea is to be found in a wider selection of non-Western and premodern societies. If progress is the evil it is often held to be, there must be something rather to admire in the societies to whom the idea never occurred. Nor am I convinced that there is merit in designating as progress every conception of the good life, improvement, development and consciousness of movement in time. As a collective singular, progress embraces all these things, but the glue holding them all together is the distinct temporal logic that offers future rewards for human action in the present.

Some may still prefer to dispense with the noun and focus instead on the nature of progressing. There are precedents to do so. While nouns or names are often elusive, verbs or actions point to observable processes. When the concept of memory has proved too thorny, scholars have opened up productive dialogues by examining how communities remember, memorialise and commemorate. When the concept of periodisation resists definition, turning attention to the action of periodising elicits discussion of how historians practically break up the past into workable chunks.

In the case of progress, to take up this proposal would be too easy a way out. Progress is not a cosmic energy thrusting humanity forward without its active participation. Better external conditions do not automatically make people better, and the political, social and cultural institutions that have developed over time to become more inclusive, representative and responsive to individual and collective initiative are not static embodiments of human progress. They are the result of unending human action, in constant need of repair, fine tuning and redefinition. History is an ongoing process and progress is the hope that our actions will take us where we decide on going.

Bibliography

Adorno, Theodor W., '"Negative" Universal History', in Rolf Tiedemann (ed.), *History and Freedom: Lectures 1964–1965*, trans. Rodney Livingstone. Cambridge: Polity Press, 2006, pp. 89–98.

Alvey, James E., 'Adam Smith's View of History: Consistent or Paradoxical?' *History of the Human Sciences* 16, 2 (2003), 1–25. https://doi.org/10.1177/0952695103016002001.

Angner, Erik, 'The History of Hayek's Theory of Cultural Evolution', *Studies in History and Philosophy of Biological and Biomedical Sciences* 33 (2002), 695–718. https://doi.org/10.1016/S1369-8486(02)00024-9.

Armitage, David, 'What's the Big Idea? Intellectual History and the Longue Durée', *History of European Ideas* 38, 4 (2012), 493–507. https://doi.org/10.1080/01916599.2012.714635.

Arndt, Heinz Wolfgang, *The Rise and Fall of Economic Growth: A Study in Contemporary Thought*. Melbourne: Longman Cheshire, 1978.

Aslanian, Sebouh David, Joyce E. Chaplin, Ann McGrath, and Kristin Mann, 'AHR *Conversation* How Size Matters: The Question of Scale in History', *American Historical Review* 118, 5 (2013), 1431–72. https://doi.org/10.1093/ahr/118.5.1431.

Bagehot, Walter, *Physics and Politics. Or Thoughts on the Application of the Principles of 'Natural Selection' and 'Inheritance' to Political Society*, 12th ed. London: Kegan Paul, Trench, Trübner, 1900. First published in 1873.

Bernstein, John Andrew, *Progress and the Quest for Meaning: A Philosophical and Historical Inquiry*. Rutherford: Fairleigh Dickinson University Press, 1993.

Blundell, Sue, *The Origins of Civilization in Greek and Roman Thought*. London: Croom Helm, 1986.

Boscov-Ellen, Dan, 'Whose Universalism? Dipesh Chakrabarty and the Anthropocene', *Capitalism Nature Socialism* 31, 1 (2020), 70–83. https://doi.org/10.1080/10455752.2018.1514060.

Briggs, Asa, *Victorian People: A Reassessment of Persons and Themes*. Chicago: University of Chicago Press, 1955.

Brynjolfsson, Erik, and Andrew McAfee, *The Second Machine Age: Work, Progress, and Prosperity in a Time of Brilliant Technologies*. New York: W. W. Norton, 2014.

Bury, John Bagnell, *The Idea of Progress: An Inquiry into Its Origin and Growth*. London: Macmillan, 1920.

Caraccioli, Louis-Antoine de, *La jouissance de soi-même*. Utrecht: E. van Harrevelt, 1759.

Chakrabarty, Dipesh, 'Anthropocene Time', *History and Theory* 57, 1 (2018), 5–32. https://doi.org/10.1111/hith.12044.

Chakrabarty, Dipesh, 'The Climate of History: Four Theses', *Critical Inquiry* 35, 2 (2009), 197–222.

Chakrabarty, Dipesh, *The Climate of History in a Planetary Age*. Chicago: University of Chicago Press, 2021.

Chandra, Bipan, *The Rise and Growth of Economic Nationalism in India: Economic Policies of Indian National Leadership, 1880–1905*. New Delhi: People's Publishing House, 1966.

Chow, Tse-tsung, *The May Fourth Movement: Intellectual Revolution in Modern China*. Cambridge, MA: Harvard University Press, 1960.

Christian, David, 'The Case for "Big History"', *Journal of World History* 2, 2 (1991), 223–38.

Christian, David, 'The Return of Universal History', *History and Theory* 49, 4 (2010), 6–27. https://doi.org/10.1111/j.1468-2303.2010.00557.x.

Clark, Christopher, *Time and Power: Visions of History in German Politics, from the Thirty Years to the Third Reich*. Princeton: Princeton University Press, 2019.

Clark, Colin, *Growthmanship: A Study in the Mythology of Investment*. London: Institute of Economic Affairs, 1961.

Cohen, Deborah, and Peter Mandler, '*The History Manifesto*: A Critique', *American Historical Review* 120, 2 (2015), 530–42. https://doi.org/10.1093/ahr/120.2.530.

Collingwood, Robin George, *An Essay on Philosophical Method*, revised ed., ed. James Connelly and Giuseppina D'Oro. Oxford: Clarendon Press, 2005. First published in 1933.

Collingwood, Robin George, *The Idea of History*, revised ed., ed. Jan van der Dussen. Oxford: Oxford University Press, 1994. First published in 1946.

Collison, Patrick, and Tyler Cowen, 'We Need a New Science of Progress: Humanity Needs to Get Better at Knowing How to Get Better', *New Atlantic*, 30 July 2019. www.theatlantic.com.

Condorcet, Jean-Antoine-Nicolas de Caritat, Marquis de, *Outlines of an Historical View of the Progress of the Human Mind*, trans. unnamed. Philadelphia: Lang and Ustick, 1796. First published in French in 1793–94.

Dale, Gareth, Manu V. Mathai, and Jose A. Puppim de Oliveira (eds.), *Green Growth: Ideology, Political Economy and the Alternatives*. London: Zed Books, 2016.

Darwin, Charles R., *On the Origin of Species by Means of Natural Selection, or the Preservation of Favoured Races in the Struggle for Life*, 3rd ed. London: John Murray, 1861.

Degérando, Joseph-Marie, *The Observation of Savage Peoples*. Abingdon: Routledge, 1969. First published in French in 1800.

DeLucia, JoEllen, *A Feminine Enlightenment: British Women Writers and the Philosophy of Progress, 1759–1820*. Edinburgh: Edinburgh University Press, 2015.

Dodds, Eric Robertson, *The Ancient Concept of Progress and Other Essays on Greek Literature and Belief*. New York: Oxford University Press, 1973.

D'Oro, Giuseppina, 'In Defence of a Humanistically Oriented Historiography: The Nature/Culture Distinction at the Time of the Anthropocene', in Jouni-Matti Kuukkanen (ed.), *Philosophy of History: Twenty-First Century Perspectives*. London: Bloomsbury Academic, 2021, pp. 216–36. https://doi.org/10.5040/9781350111875.0019.

Edelstein, Ludwig, *The Idea of Progress in Classical Antiquity*. Baltimore: Johns Hopkins University Press, 1967.

Fagan, Madeleine, 'On the Dangers of an Anthropocene Epoch: Geological Time, Political Time and Post-Human Politics', *Political Geography* 70 (2019), 55–63. https://doi.org/10.1016/j.polgeo.2019.01.008.

Fischer, Louis (ed.), *The Essential Gandhi: His Life, Work, and Ideas; an Anthology*. New York: Vintage Books, 1963.

Fourastié, Jean, *Les Trente glorieuses, ou La révolution invisible de 1946 à 1975*. Paris: Fayard, 1979.

Freeden, Michael, *The New Liberalism: An Ideology of Social Reform*. Oxford: Oxford University Press, 1978.

Friedman, Milton, 'Neoliberalism and Its Prospects', *Farmand* 17 (1951), 89–94.

Furth, Charlotte, 'May Fourth in History', in Benjamin J. Schwartz (ed.), *Reflections on the May Fourth Movement: A Symposium*. Cambridge, MA: Harvard University Press, 1972, pp. 59–68.

Gallicchio, Marc, *The African American Encounter with Japan and China*. Chapel Hill: University of North Carolina Press, 2000.

Ge, Zhaoguang, *An Intellectual History of China, Volume 1: Knowledge, Thought and Belief before the Seventh Century CE*, trans. Michael S. Duke and Josephine Chiu-Duke. Leiden: Brill, 2014.

González-Reimann, Luis, *The Mahābhārata and the Yugas: India's Great Epic Poem and the Hindu System of World Ages*. New York: Peter Lang, 2002.

Gordon, Robert J., *Rise and Fall of American Growth: The U.S. Standard of Living since the Civil War*. Princeton: Princeton University Press, 2016.

Gramelsberger, Gabriele, 'From Science to Computational Sciences: A Science History and Philosophy Overview', in Gabriele Gramelsberger (ed.), *Studies in the History of Computing and Its Influence on Today's Sciences*. Zurich: Diaphanes, 2011, pp. 19–44.

Green, Karen, *A History of Women's Political Thought in Europe, 1700–1800*. Cambridge: Cambridge University Press, 2014.

Guldi, Jo, and David Armitage, *The History Manifesto*. Cambridge: Cambridge University Press, 2014.

Haff, Peter, 'The Technosphere and Its Relation to the Anthropocene', in Jan Zalasiewicz, Colin N. Waters, Mark Williams and Colin P. Summerhayes (eds.), *The Anthropocene as a Geological Time Unit: A Guide to the Scientific Evidence and Current Debate*. Cambridge: Cambridge University Press, 2019, pp. 138–43. https://doi.org/10.1017/9781108621359.

Hare, J. Laurence, and Fabian Link, 'The Idea of *Volk* and the Origins of *Völkisch* Research, 1800–1930s', *Journal of the History of Ideas* 80, 4 (2019), 575–96. https://doi.org/10.1353/jhi.2019.0032.

Hartog, François, 'The Modern *Régime* of Historicity in the Face of Two World Wars', in Chris Lorenz and Berber Bevernage (eds.), *Breaking Up Time: Negotiating the Borders between Past, Present and Future*. Göttingen: Vandenhoeck and Ruprecht, 2013, pp. 124–33.

Hawkins, Mike, 'Social Darwinism and Race', in Stefan Berger (ed.), *A Companion to Nineteenth-Century Europe, 1789–1914*. Oxford: Blackwell, 2006, pp. 224–35.

Hawkins, Mike, *Social Darwinism in European and American Thought, 1860–1945: Nature as Model and Nature as Threat*. Cambridge: Cambridge University Press, 1997.

Hay, James Roy, *The Origins of the Liberal Welfare Reforms 1906–1914*. London: Macmillan, 1975.

Hayek, Friedrich A., *The Fatal Conceit: The Errors of Socialism*. London: Routledge, 1988.

Hayek, Friedrich A., *Law, Legislation and Liberty: A New Statement of the Liberal Principles of Justice, Volume 3: The Political Order of a Free People*. London: Routledge and Kegan Paul, 1979.

Hayek, Friedrich A., *The Road to Serfdom*. London: Routledge, 2001. First published in 1944.

Hegel, Georg Wilhelm Friedrich, *The Philosophy of Right* and *the Philosophy of History*, 2nd ed., trans. Thomas Malcolm Knox and John Sibree. Chicago: Encyclopædia Britannica, 1990.

Heidegger, Martin, *The Concept of Time*, trans. William McNeill. Oxford: Blackwell, 1992. First published in German in 1924.

Heilbroner, Robert L., 'The Paradox of Progress: Decline and Decay in the Wealth of Nations', *Journal of the History of Ideas* 34, 2 (1973), 243–62. https://doi.org/10.2307/2708728.

Hirsch, Fred, *Social Limits to Growth*. London: Routledge, 1995. First published in 1977.

Hobhouse, Leonard Trelawny, *Liberalism*. Oxford: Oxford University Press, 1911.

Hölscher, Lucian, 'Mysteries of Historical Order: Ruptures, Simultaneity, and the Relationship of the Past, the Present and the Future', in Chris Lorenz and Berber Bevernage (eds.), *Breaking Up Time: Negotiating the Borders between Past, Present and Future*. Göttingen: Vandenhoeck and Ruprecht, 2013, pp. 134–51.

Hughes-Warrington, Marnie, with Anne Martin, *Big and Little Histories: Sizing Up Ethics in Historiography*. London: Routledge, 2022.

Hume, David, 'The Rise of the Arts and the Progress of Science', in *Essays, Political, and Literary*. Indianapolis: Liberty Fund, 1985, pp. 111–37. First published in 1777.

Jackson, Tim, *Prosperity without Growth: Economics for a Finite Planet*. Abingdon: Earthscan, 2009.

Jacobs, Struan, and Ian Tregenza, 'Rationalism and Tradition: The Popper-Oakeshott Conversation', *European Journal of Political Theory* 13, 1 (2014), 3–24. https://doi.org/10.1177/1474885112471274.

Jaspers, Karl, *The Origin and Goal of History*. New Haven: Yale University Press, 1953. First published in German in 1949.

Jerven, Morten, *Poor Numbers: How We Are Misled by African Development Statistics and What to Do About It*. Ithaca: Cornell University Press, 2013.

Johnson, Harriet, 'Anthropocene as a Negative Universal History', *Adorno Studies* 3, 1 (2019), 49–63.

Jordheim, Helge, and Einar Wigen, 'Conceptual Synchronisation: From Progress to Crisis', *Millennium: Journal of International Studies* 46, 3 (2018), 421–39. https://doi.org/10.1177/0305829818774781.

Kant, Immanuel, 'Anthropology from a Pragmatic Point of View', in Robert B. Louden and Günter Zöller (eds.), *Anthropology, History, and Education*, trans. Robert B. Louden. Cambridge: Cambridge University Press, 2007, pp. 227–429. First published in German in 1798.

Kant, Immanuel, 'Idea for a Universal History with a Cosmopolitan Purpose'; 'The Contest of Faculties'; 'Perpetual Peace: A Philosophical Sketch', in Hans Reiss (ed.), *Kant: Political Writings*, 2nd ed., trans. Hugh Barr. Nisbet. Cambridge: Cambridge University Press, 1991, pp. 41–53, 177–90, 93–130.

Karabell, Zachary, *The Leading Indicators: A Short History of the Numbers that Rule Our World*. Riverside: Simon and Schuster, 2014.

Kidd, Benjamin, *Social Evolution*. London: Macmillan, 1896.

Kirk, Geoffrey Stephen, John Earle Raven, and Malcolm Schofield, *The Presocratic Philosophers: A Critical History with a Selection of Texts*, 2nd ed. Cambridge: Cambridge University Press, 1983.

Kitcher, Philip, with Jan-Christoph Heilinger, Rahel Jaeggi, and Susan Neiman, *Moral Progress*, ed. Amia Srinivasan. Oxford: Oxford University Press, 2021.

Koselleck, Reinhart, *Futures Past: On the Semantics of Historical Time*, trans. Keith Tribe. Cambridge, MA: MIT Press, 1985.

Koselleck, Reinhart, 'Introduction and Prefaces to the *Geschichtliche Grundbegriffe*' (trans. Michaela Richter), *Contributions to the History of Concepts* 6, 1 (2011), 1–37. https://doi.org/10.3167/choc.2011.060102.

Koselleck, Reinhart, Werner Conze, and Otto Brunner (eds.), *Geschichtliche Grundbegriffe: Historisches Lexikon zur politisch-sozialen Sprache in Deutschland*, Volume 2. Stuttgart: Klett-Cotta, 1975.

Krieger, Leonard, 'The Idea of Progress', *The Review of Metaphysics* 4, 4 (1951), 483–94.

Last, Angela, 'We Are the World? Anthropocene Cultural Production between Geopoetics and Geopolitics', *Theory, Culture & Society* 34, 2–3 (2017), 147–68. https://doi.org/10.1177/0263276415598626.

Le Goff, Jacques, *Must We Divide History into Periods?* trans. *M. B. DeBevoise*. New York: Columbia University Press, 2015.

Levenson, J. C., 'Writing History in the Age of Darwin', *Raritan* 23, 3 (2004), 115–48.

Macaulay, Catharine, *A Treatise on the Immutability of Moral Truth*. London: A. Hamilton, 1783.

Macekura, Stephen J., *The Mismeasure of Progress: Economic Growth and Its Critics*. Chicago: University of Chicago Press, 2020.

Macintyre, Stuart, *Australia's Boldest Experiment: War and Reconstruction in the 1940s*. Sydney: NewSouth, 2015.

Mandeville, Bernard, *The Fable of the Bees: Or, Private Vices, Publick Benefits*, Volume 1, ed. Frederick Benjamin Kaye. Oxford: Clarendon Press, 1924.

Manuel, Frank E., *The Prophets of Paris*. New York: Harper Torchbooks, 1965.

Marcell, David D., *Progress and Pragmatism: James, Dewey, Beard, and the American Idea of Progress*. Westport: Greenwood Press, 1974.

Martin, Tony, *Marcus Garvey, Hero: A First Biography*. Dover: Majority Press, 1983.

Marx, Karl, *Capital*, 2nd ed., ed. Friedrich Engels, trans. Samuel Moore and Edward Aveling. Chicago: Encyclopædia Britannica, 1990. Translated from third German ed.

Maynard, John, *Fight for Liberty and Freedom: The Origins of Australian Aboriginal Activism*. Canberra: Aboriginal Studies Press, 2007.

McNeill, John Robert, *Something New under the Sun: An Environmental History of the Twentieth-Century World*. New York: W. W. Norton, 2001.

Meek, Ronald L., *Turgot on Progress, Sociology and Economics*. Cambridge: Cambridge University Press, 1973.

Melnik, Denis V., 'Lenin as a Development Economist: A Study in Application of Marx's Theory in Russia', *Russian Journal of Economics* 7 (2021), 34–49. https://doi.org/10.32609/j.ruje.7.57963.

Mende, Tibor, *Conversations with Mr. Nehru*. London: Secker and Warburg, 1956.

Millar, John, *The Origin of the Distinction of Ranks; or, an Inquiry into the Circumstances which Give Rise to Influence and Authority in the Different Members of Society*. London: J. Murray, 1779.

Miller, Riel, 'Futures Literacy: Transforming the Future', in Riel Miller (ed.), *Transforming the Future: Anticipation in the 21st Century*. London: Routledge, 2018, pp. 1–12.

Moynihan, Thomas, 'Existential Risk and Human Extinction: An Intellectual History', *Futures* 116 (2020), 1–13.

Muraca, Barbara, 'Décroissance: A Project for a Radical Transformation of Society', *Environmental Values* 22, 2 (2013), 147–69. https://doi.org/10.3197/096327113X13581561725112.

Myrdal, Gunnar, *Asian Drama: An Inquiry into the Poverty of Nations*, Volume 1. Harmondsworth: Penguin Books, 1968.

Nakayama, Shigeru, 'The Chinese "Cyclic" View of History vs. Japanese "Progress"', in Arnold Burgen, Peter McLaughlin and Jürgen Mittelstrass (eds.), *The Idea of Progress*. Berlin: De Gruyter, 1997, pp. 65–76. https://doi.org/10.1515/9783110820423.65.

Naoroji, Dadabhai, *Poverty and Un-British Rule in India*. New Delhi: Commonwealth, 1901.

Nehru, Jawaharlal, *Glimpses of World History: Being Further Letters to His Daughter, Written in Prison, and Containing a Rambling Account of History for Young People*. Delhi: Oxford University Press, 1982. First published in 1934.

Nelson, William Max, *The Time of Enlightenment: Constructing the Future in France, 1750 to Year One*. Toronto: University of Toronto Press, 2021.

Nisbet, Robert A., *History of the Idea of Progress*. London: Routledge, 2017. First published in 1980.

Nordblad, Julia, 'On the Difference between Anthropocene and Climate Change Temporalities', *Critical Inquiry* 48, 2 (2021), 328–48.

Oakeshott, Michael, *On Human Conduct*. Oxford: Oxford University Press, 1975.

Oakeshott, Michael, *Rationalism in Politics and Other Essays*. Indianapolis: Liberty Fund, 1991.

O'Brien, Karen, *Women and Enlightenment in Eighteenth-Century Britain*. Cambridge: Cambridge University Press, 2009.

OECD, *Statistics, Knowledge and Policy: OECD World Forum on Key Indicators*. Paris: OECD, 2005.

Passmore, John, *The Perfectibility of Man*, 3rd ed. Indianapolis: Liberty Fund, 2000. First published in 1970.

Peck, Jamie, *Constructions of Neoliberal Reason*. Oxford: Oxford University Press, 2010.

Popper, Karl R., *The Logic of Scientific Discovery*. London: Routledge, 1992. First published in German in 1934.

Popper, Karl R., *The Open Society and Its Enemies*, 5th ed. London: Routledge, 2002. First published in 1945.

Popper, Karl R., *The Poverty of Historicism*. London: Routledge and Kegan Paul, 1957.

Powell, Barry B., *The Poems of Hesiod: Theogony, Works and Days, and the Shield of Herakles*. Oakland: University of California Press, 2017.

Purushotham, Sunil, 'World History in the Atomic Age: Past, Present and Future in the Political Thought of Jawaharlal Nehru', *Modern Intellectual History* 14, 3 (2017), 837–67. https://doi.org/10.1017/S1479244316000093.

Ranelagh, John, *Thatcher's People: An Insider's Account of the Politics, the Power and the Personalities*. London: HarperCollins, 1991.

Rousseau, Jean-Jacques, *The Social Contract and the First and Second Discourses*. New Haven: Yale University Press, 2002.

Royer, Clémence, Preface to *De l'origine des espèces par sélection naturelle ou des lois de transformation des êtres organisés*, 3rd ed., trans. Clémence Royer. Paris: Guillaumin et Cie, Victor Masson et Fils, 1870.

Ruse, Michael, *Evolution as Religion: What Literature Tells Us About Evolution*. Oxford: Oxford University Press, 2017.

Ruse, Michael, *Monad to Man: The Concept of Progress in Evolutionary Biology*. Cambridge, MA: Harvard University Press, 2009.

Schmelzer, Matthias, *The Hegemony of Growth: The OECD and the Making of the Economic Growth Paradigm*. Cambridge: Cambridge University Press, 2016.

Scott, David, *Conscripts of Modernity: The Tragedy of Colonial Enlightenment*. Durham: Duke University Press, 2004.

Sen, Amartya, *On Economic Inequality.* Oxford: Oxford University Press, 1973.

Sihvola, Juha, *Decay, Progress, the Good Life? Hesiod and Protagoras on the Development of Culture.* Helsinki: Finnish Society of Sciences and Letters, 1989.

Simon, Zoltán Boldizsár, *History in Times of Unprecedented Change: A Theory for the 21st Century.* London: Bloomsbury Academic, 2019.

Simon, Zoltán Boldizsár, and Lars Deile (eds.), *Historical Understanding: Past, Present, and Future.* London: Bloomsbury Academic, 2022.

Slaboch, Matthew, *A Road to Nowhere: The Idea of Progress and Its Critics.* Philadelphia: University of Pennsylvania Press, 2017.

Slaboch, Matthew, 'Tocqueville's Philosophy of History: Its Meaning and Implications for Russia and Central and Eastern Europe', in Peter Boettke and Adam Martin (eds.), *Exploring the Social and Political Economy of Alexis de Tocqueville.* London: Palgrave, 2020, pp. 83–99. https://doi.org/10.1007/978-3-030-34937-0_5.

Smith, Gary (ed.), *Benjamin: Philosophy, Aesthetics, History.* Chicago: University of Chicago Press, 1989.

Sorel, Georges, *The Illusions of Progress.* Berkeley: University of California Press, 1969. First published in French in 1908.

Spadafora, David, *The Idea of Progress in Eighteenth-Century Britain.* New Haven: Yale University Press, 1990.

Speich, Daniel, 'The Use of Global Abstractions: National Income Accounting and the Period of Imperial Decline', *Journal of Global History* 6 (2011), 7–28. https://doi.org/10.1017/S1740022811000027.

Stiglitz, Joseph, 'If Olaf Scholz is Serious about Progress, He Must Back a Patent Waiver for Covid Vaccines', *Guardian*, 15 December 2021. www.theguardian.com.

Swyngedouw, Erik, 'The Non-Political Politics of Climate Change', *ACME: An International Journal for Critical Geographies* 12, 1 (2013), 1–8.

Tocqueville, Alexis de, *The Old Régime and the French Revolution*, trans. Stuart Gilbert. Garden City: Anchor Books, 1955. First published in French in 1856.

Traver, Guillermo Galbe, 'Hayek's View of History: A Critique and a Proposal', *Laissez-Faire* 46 (2017), 25–30.

Vyverberg, Henry, *Historical Pessimism in the French Enlightenment.* Cambridge, MA: Harvard University Press, 1958.

Wang, Jessica Ching-Sze, *John Dewey in China: To Teach and to Learn.* Albany: State University of New York Press, 2007.

Wang, Q. Edward, *Inventing China through History: A May Fourth Approach to Historiography.* Albany: State University of New York Press, 2000.

Weiss, Richard S., *Emergence of Modern Hinduism: Religion on the Margins of Colonialism*. Berkeley: University of California Press, 2019.

West, Martin Litchfield, Translator's Introduction to Hesiod's *Theogony* and *Works and Days*. Oxford: Oxford University Press, 1988.

Wittner, David G., *Technology and the Culture of Progress in Meiji Japan*. Abingdon: Routledge, 2008.

Acknowledgements

I am grateful to the Department of Philosophy, Classics, History of Art and Ideas at the University of Oslo, where a three-month stay in 2021 enabled me to read, write and present my ideas. I should single out Tor Egil Førland, Matthew Kinloch, Christine Amadou, Ellen Krefting, Håkon Evju and Øystein Linnebo, as well as my hosts at several guest lectures associated with the project: Liisi Keedus, Johan Östling, James Connelly, Maria Grever, Robbert-Jan Adriaansen, Alejandra Mancilla and Helge Jordheim. Daniel Woolf edited with alacrity. Gitte Westergaard was by my side the entire time.

In memory of Stuart Macintyre (1947–2021), historian, who lived with purpose

Cambridge Elements꞊

Historical Theory and Practice

Printed in the United States
by Baker & Taylor Publisher Services